WORLD BUILDING THROUGH CULTURE

A Workbook for Storytellers

Copyright © 2022 by **J.M. Frey**

ISBN 978-1-7778107-1-9 (ppbk)

All rights reserved. No part of this publication may be reproduced, distributed transmitted in any form or by any means, without prior written permission.

Cover Design © 2022 J.M. Frey
Interior Design © 2022 J.M. Frey
Published with IngramSpark
www.jmfrey.net

For Ruthanne Reid,

An amazing friend and creator, who is always generous with her Time, Talent, and Wisdom, and whose dedication to her Craft should be an inspiration to writers everywhere.

FOR KIM ANNE FIELD,

AN AMAZING FRIEND AND CREATOR, WHO IS ALWAYS
GENEROUS WITH HER TIME, TALENT, AND WISDOM, AND
WHOSE DEDICATION TO HER CRAFT IS SOMETHING I WILL
ENDEAVOR TO LIVE UP TO EVERY DAY.

Table of Contents

How to Use This Workbook	1
Introduction To Culturebuilding	5
Finding your Starting Point	31
The Big Questions	38
The Small Questions	55
The Sliding Scale	313
Language and Dialogue	318
Character Sketches	338
Notes	363
About the Author	380

How To Use This Workbook

Welcome! Thank you for purchasing this workbook. You're probably planning to use it to create a rich and detailed secondary story world. I'm happy to be here to help!

The book itself is supplied with blank spaces to make notes directly on the pages themselves. Please, write in it. Doodle. Scribble. Scratch things out. Erase. Staple things in. This is meant to be a *work* book in every possible way. And there's no rule saying you have to go in order, either, if you don't want to.

Contents

This workbook is made up of eight parts:

- An introduction to worldbuilding through culture.
- A discussion about internal, unconscious bias meant to help you step back from your own cultural context. I'll encourage you to investigate the beliefs and systems around you that seem to be natural, but are actually societal constructs.
- An overview of the Four Big Questions, whose answers will form the basis of your created culture.
- A series of questions and thought exercises to help you drill down into the nitty-gritty realities of your imagined culture.
- A section that allows you to mark where the values of your society sit on a binary sliding scale.

- A section on oral/written communication to help you form verbal tics, idioms, and speech patterns that will help flesh out your culture and give it a unique sound.
- A space for character sketches, where you can record your characters' relationships to the culture you've created for them to inhabit, and make notes about their individual appearances and preferences.
- Blank pages where you can make your own notes.

This workbook is the perfect place to keep all these musings, thoughts, reasons, and descriptions, outside of the Manuscript, eliminating the need to infodump in the book itself. Then you'll have it all in one place, easy to read at a glance, and ready to remind you what you've decided. It's also easily added to, or changed, as the story, and therefore character and world, evolve and come together.

Not Simply a "Yes" or "No"

When answering each question, I encourage you to provide details that will help you flesh out your world. Give not only the facts of the societal custom / taboo / law you're creating, but also the *Who, What, Where, When, Why* of it.

While most of the questions can be answered with a simple "yes" or "no", don't stop there. With every answer you record, ask yourself three more:

1. What is the historical precedent / genesis of this rule/custom/taboo? Where did it *come* from?
2. How is it enforced / recognized / celebrated among the *most* privileged people in society. What impact does it have on their daily lives?
3. How is it enforced / recognized / celebrated among the *least* privileged people in society. What impact does it have on their daily lives?

WORLDBUILDING THROUGH CULTURE

Provide the 5Ws, but also write down the answers to these +3 extra questions. I've left space for you to do so on each page.

5W+3 Example

In most current Western societies, driving your car too fast is punishable by a monetary fine.

Who:
This law applies to all operators of motor vehicles.

What:
Speed limits are set by local governments, based on the historical usage pattern of that particular road, whether it caters to pedestrians or cyclists as well as motor vehicles, the width of the road, if there are any businesses, parking, schools, hospitals, or homes on the road, and how people use the road today.

Where:
On all publicly funded and maintained roadways.

When:
At all times. However, a driver must be caught in the act of speeding (either by a camera or law enforcement officer) for the fine to be applied.

Why:
Speed limits are set and enforced to prevent accidents. This is a measure to prevent loss of life, medical emergencies, and property damage (all of which would use up taxpayer money to repair, to transport the injured, and to provide them with medical care.)

Precedent / Genesis:
Car accidents have been happening since cars shared the roadway with horses. As motors got more powerful and cars gained the ability to go faster, local governments created bylaws to regulate the flow of

traffic and prevent accidents (and prevent government spending on medical care and infrastructure repair).

Most Privileged:
For those with wealth, the amount of the monetary fine is negligible, and therefore may not be a strong deterrent. This may lead to wealthy citizens disregarding laws flagrantly, frequently, and casually. The power and position accompanying their wealth may also lead to less jail time or legal penalty if they injure / kill someone, or create property damage.

Least Privileged:
For those with little money, the fine may equal their budget for the month, and they therefore cannot afford to get caught speeding. Additionally, the loss or damage of their vehicle may negatively impact their ability to work, putting them in further financial straits. Therefore, the least privileged are more likely to adhere to laws.

Now that we have an overview of how and why these laws exist, imagine how your main character would react if they were caught speeding. Based on their socio-economic background, class, ethnicity, or any other metric by which you stratify your society, how severe will the punishment be for your character? How will the law enforcement officer react to them, and behave around them? How fairly will the law be applied to your character if they're a recognizable public figure—will they get away with it, or will they be extra-punished for setting a bad example?

While it seems like a lot of thinking to do for a relatively simple thing like a speeding fine, having a deep and thorough understanding of the laws, taboos, morals, and expectations of the society you're building will make your world—and the story featuring it—believable, internally consistent, and engaging.

Introduction to Culturebuilding

Culture is not Geography

When making up a new place to set a story, writers often focus on the physical setting first: what level of urbanization the place where your characters live is, what the trees are like, how the seasons shift and flow into one another, how close it is to the sea or the mountains, how cold it gets at night, etc. These factors–geography and climate–all feed into the foundation and development of a fictional culture, but they aren't a culture in and of itself.

There's nothing at all wrong with starting on the tangibilities of a book's setting. I like a good map as much as the next fantasy writer. But once you've got that settled, you need to look at how they directly impact the traditions, taboos, and values of your fictional culture.

Building a robust and believable culture is a vital storytelling practice, because it will influence every aspect of your characters' personalities, choices, and journey. The morals they hold, the taboos they rail against, the rules they enforce or break, their favourite foods, and clothes, and sayings–these are all cultural.

Unlike geography and climate, which are naturally occurring, a culture is an artificial, ever-evolving construct. Geography and climate influence a culture, but they are not a culture in and of themselves.

For example, an equatorial climate where it grows so unbearably hot at midday that humans and animals get sleepy is *geography* and *climate*. Choosing to shut up the shops for a few hours around noon so folks can nap and relax, and then resuming day-to-day life after the sun has set and it's cooler, is *cultural*.

Yet you'll note that not every society that experiences drowsy-inducing midday heat practices the art of the siesta. Other cultures around the world may share the same latitudes, but not the same attitudes.

Drowsy-making heat is climate; *siesta* is culture.

The Cultural Iceberg

A culture dictates the way people behave around one another; what is considered polite and acceptable, or not. A culture influences what people eat, how they prepare it, and the etiquette around consuming it. A culture influences what people wear, what trendy fashions they follow, and what is considered acceptable clothing in terms of gender, sex, or occupation. A culture dictates the laws and rules of interpersonal relationships, and societal responsibility.

Culture, in short, is the *why* behind everything we do, think, and believe. The internal, unseen reasons for *why* we do things a certain way, or hold specific values. Those *why*s then influence and bubble up into the visible area of the culture as *how*s, *when*s, and *where*s.

If we were to compare a culture to an iceberg, then what you'd see above the water line of a culture is an outward manifestation of the things that make up the base of the culture, below the waterline. It is easy to see, taste, hear, experience and emulate what is above the waterline (the *what* and *how* of the culture) but far more difficult to easily and quickly comprehend what is below it (the *why*.)

WORLDBUILDING THROUGH CULTURE

Graph of The Cultural Iceberg[1]

THE SEEN

Behaviors & Practices

Architecture
Music
Food
Fashion
Language
Literature & Poetry
Fine Art
Dress
Games
Holidays & Festivals

The Conscious

The Unconscious

Perceptions
Attitudes
Beliefs
Values
Economics
Media
Education
Ideology & Religion

Etiquette
Learning Styles
Patterns of Speech
Body Language
Traditions
Social Hierarchies
Assumptions
Politics
Notions of Modesty
Nature of Friendship
Concept of Fairness
Importance of Space
Gender Roles
Notions of 'Self'
Religious Beliefs & Practices

THE UNSEEN

---

[1] Adapted from the graphic in:
Hall, Edward T. *Beyond Culture*. (Doubleday, 1976).

Culture is an umbrella term which encompasses the social behavior, institutions, and norms found in human societies from or attributed to a specific region or location. It includes the knowledge, beliefs, arts, laws, customs, capabilities, cuisines, dress, and habits of the individuals in these groups.

A great shorthand for understanding this sort of seen/unseen divide is to think of your favourite Regency Era-set television program or film. It's easy to make things *look* Regency. You just need some empire-waist dresses, fancy assembly rooms, bonnets, high-necked waistcoats, carriages, Georgian architecture and, of course, an establishing shot of The Circus in Bath. Harder to convey on the screen is the *why* behind those stereotypical visual choices.

Did you know that Henrietta Howard, the Duchess of Suffolk (1689-1767), popularized the very Greek-looking, evenly-spaced facades of Georgian architecture with Marble Hill House, which she designed herself? The house was influenced by her personal love of Palladian architecture, which was one of the houses that started the trend. Why was she an influencer of the era? Because she was King George II's mistress and was in Queen Caroline's entourage. She dressed the queen, and so had a large influence on the fashion of the time. As a friend and patroness of great minds and artists of the day, her personal fondness for Classical Greek-inspired clothing, architecture, silhouettes, philosophies and critical thinking eventually filtered into contemporary pop culture[2]. Though, as it *was* the eighteenth century, things filtered a lot more slowly than they do today.

George II was, of course, the father of George III, whose struggles with mental illness were the reason that *his* son, George IV, needed to become the Regent while George III still lived, giving the cultural era its name. What we think of the above-the-water-line 'Regency Era'

---

[2] Borman, Tracy. *King's Mistress, Queen's Servant: The Life and Times of Henrietta Howard*. (Random House, 2008).

can nearly entirely be traced back to the personal taste of a woman who died a decade before Jane Austen was born.

Culture is therefore everything that makes your society feel, think, behave, travel, worship, believe, taste, smell, and sound like *itself*, both tangibly and intangibly.

Think about where you live—and what about your particular culture is both similar and different from the one of your country's nearest neighbour.

That is culture.

Regional Differences

Rarely are cultures homogenous. That is, not every region within the same country or climate is going to be the exact same. The influences of neighbouring cultures may seep into a region on a border, or different climates within the same kingdom, state, or nation may influence fashion, food, and morals. Laws may be the same across a nation, but taboos and traditions may be different in each area.

For example, while both are provinces in the country of Canada, the province of Newfoundland (maritime) and the province of Saskatchewan (prairie) have differing local cultures.

The contemporary culture of Newfoundland grew out of the harsh, rocky landscape and proximity to the North Atlantic. It is a product of the historic sealing, maritime, and fishing industries, and the traditions of the early predominantly Portuguese, French, and Celtic European Settlers.

Whereas early settlers into Saskatchewan were mostly Eastern European or Scandinavian, founding homesteads and towns on fertile plains. The economic platform of the province is based in the ranching and agricultural industries, so the cuisine, music culture, and fashion is obviously going to be different from that of Newfoundland, even though they are both within the same country.

That's not even taking into account the cultures of the advanced Indigenous societies that colonialism in both of these provinces disrupted and / or destroyed. Early settlers would have learned much of adapting to their new climate from their First Nations neighbours, folding that knowledge into their own culture and adopting practices and cuisines, modes of dress, and ways of building shelter.

Based on the climate, available natural resources and foods, backgrounds, and cultural heritage of the people who live in each of these provinces, you can guess how their cuisine, music, and traditional dress may differ.

It would be the same in any fictional culture you create—different landscapes and neighbours will lead to different variations on the same base culture.

Culturebuilding and Maps

Okay, so world and culturebuilding may be more than just maps, but the maps are important, too. Geography and climate have their own unique influence on the genesis of a culture. Access to water, agriculture, hunting, fishing, plants for textiles, natural shelter, materials to build shelter, the harshness of the temperatures and seasonal changes, etc., all of these things have a direct impact on how and why specific aspects of your created culture exist as they do.

Going back to our Canadian provinces example, it's natural for a culture located on a rocky island with little pastureland like Newfoundland to have a cuisine that focuses heavily on seafood, fruit and vegetables that don't require a lot of arable land to grow (such as blueberries and tubers) and animals that can be raised without grazing, like poultry. And because this would make something like beef very expensive to raise or import, it becomes a special-occasion food, or a mark of high status or wealth. Conversely, in Saskatchewan, where significant portions of the arable land is given over for cattle ranching and cash crop, but the ocean is very far away, the status of cuisine could be assumed to be inverted. Beef is local and cheap, and fish and seafood must be imported and becomes the wealth-indicator or special-occasion meal.

Deciding *where* your culture is located geographically is quite important to the foundation of the culture itself. When creating your culture, consider the historic origins of the settlement and community. How long have these people lived here? Was there another settlement there first, which was abandoned and they built on? Or were there people living there already? If so, did your culture invade, or did they sneak in, or were they invited? Is it subsequently a melting pot culture, or are there clear divisions between cultural neighbourhoods and backgrounds?

Also ask yourself: why settle *here* specifically?

If you look at the locations of most major cities–especially capitals–you'll see that they have several things in common:

- Easy access to fresh water.
- Access to food sources; either good agricultural land, or abundant sea stocks, or plains and forests where food naturally grows and wild animals thrive, or a combination of the above.
- Access to building materials; an abundance of clay for adobe architecture, or stone to quarry, or wood for timber, etc.
- Access to materials to make clothing from; either hides and furs, or plants like cotton and hemp, or supple and weaveable grasses or tree barks, etc.
- Access and (more importantly), *control* of trade routes, ports and terminals, and markets. (What *has* to come through your city, in order to get to other places? What do your people have access to that they can trade / sell so their community thrives? How do they center or celebrate that commodity in their culture and festivals?)

Once you've figured out the where and the why of your culture's settlement (or non-settlement, if they are a culture that follows the resources as they move), it's time to name it.

As fun as it is to give places grand names that sound fantastical and will be the bane of your audiobook narrator's day, remember that humans tend to be extremely literal when it comes to naming places. I mean, the name of our planet is "Dirt".

Take a look at a map of your country, and see which names you can easily categorize by:

- Geographical Location or Notable Features
  - Big Hill, Little Falls, Forks, etc.
- Renamed from other languages
  - For example, there are so many rivers named Avon in the U.K. because the Ancient Celtic word for river was 'avon', and when the mapmakers of Rome asked the locals the name of the river, they replied: "the river."
- Named after someone or something important
  - For example, Trafalgar Road in southern Ontario is named after Trafalgar Square in London, England, which is named in honour of the Battle of Trafalgar, which is so named because it took place close to Cape Trafalgar, which itself is a bastardization of the original Arabic name for the promontory: Taraf al-Ghar (طرف الغار 'cape of the cave/laurel'), or from Taraf al-Gharb (طرف الغرب 'cape of the west')[3]
- Named after a place where folks used to live before
  - They may do this by adding 'new' to it, to differentiate from the 'old' (New York,

---

[3] "Cape Trafalgar". *Wikipedia.org* <https://en.wikipedia.org/wiki/Cape_Trafalgar> Accessed: 06/27/2022.

New Orleans, New Zealand,) or they may just use the placename as-is (Scarborough, Ontario, Canada is named for Scarborough, North Yorkshire, England).

There's lots of map-building software and websites out there—and of course, drawing supplies so you can make your own physical version. Or you can do what I did for my fantasy series—trace around a coffee stain on a napkin, start roughing in mountains and rivers, and go from there.

Don't forget that your character will be leaving this place (either physically or metaphorically) to begin their adventure, so think about what they take with them that is important to their home culture, but may be useless or weird in the wider world. Or, conversely, extremely helpful if other characters have never seen the thing before.

Rough Map of Your World

Culturebuilding and the Hero's Journey

The usefulness and universality of Joseph Campbell's Hero's Journey[4] monomyth plot cycle is arguable, but you can't deny that it's pervasive. Campbell studied Western myths, fairy tales, folklore, religions, and other forms of shared narratives to discover if there were any commonalities in them. From that, he synthesized the tales, and created a simple step-by-step understanding of the stories of classical mythic heroes like Osiris, Jesus Christ, and Odysseus. The resulting book, *The Hero with a Thousand Faces*, published in 1949, has influenced creative writing and storytelling across the contemporary Western world ever since. (Most notably, George Lucas' *Star Wars*[5].)

Campbell's Hero's Journey is a narrative archetype, or story template. It follows a protagonist-hero who leaves home, goes on an adventure, learns a lesson, wins a victory with their newfound knowledge, and then returns home transformed.

The Twelve Steps of the Hero's Journey:

ACT I - SEPARATION

- The Ordinary World

Peacefully rooted in their home culture, the hero is lacking something, or has something taken from them.

---

[4] Campbell, Joseph. *The Hero with a Thousand Faces*. (Pantheon Books, 1968).

[5] Searson, Hannah. "Star Wars and The Hero With a Thousand Faces: Why does Joseph Campbell's influence on Star Wars matter?" *Joseph Campbell Foundation*, 01/06/2020. <https://jcf.org/notes/star-wars-and-the-hero-with-a-thousand-faces/> Accessed: 10/24/2022.

- The Call to Adventure

The hero blunders into a challenge, problem, or adventure by chance. (Or at least, it *appears* to be by chance in Chosen One narratives.)

- Refusing the Call

The hero leaves home, often reluctantly, to pursue what they are lacking, or what was taken. The motivation to achieve their goal eventually outweighs their reluctance.

- Meeting the Mentor

The hero encounters a wise and / or experienced person, or enchanted object, who motivates the hero and prepares the hero to continue their journey. This mentor gives advice, guidance, or an item, but cannot go with the hero. The mentor either remains behind or dies.

ACT II - INITIATION

- Crossing the Threshold

All reluctance gone, the hero commits to their task, and enters a special world, new reality, or other realm. They are often challenged by a threshold guardian of some sort.

- Tests, Allies, and Enemies

The hero learns the rules of this new world by meeting people, and obtaining new information. The hero collects allies. The hero's true character is tested and revealed, and their innermost truths exposed.

- Approaching the Innermost Cave

The hero and their allies near the end of their journey, and are at the edge of the place where the object of their quest resides. This often involves crossing into a literal or metaphorical Realm of the Dead.

- The Supreme Ordeal

The hero faces unspeakable danger, often a life-or-death struggle that is either physical or psychological, and generally acts as the climax of the plot.

- Seizing the Reward

After surviving, our hero takes possession of the object of the quest, (typically another person, a treasure, a weapon, or specific knowledge) or achieves a reconciliation with someone.

ACT III - THE RETURN

- The Road Back

Fleeing, the hero must now deal with the consequences of their actions. They may be pursued by remaining antagonists or forces. The hero faces the decision to return to the ordinary world, or remain in the special one.

- Resurrection

In one final psychological or physical test, the hero is able to leave the special realm. This generally manifests as an emotional, mental or physical resurrection, purification, rebirth, or miraculous transformation.

- Returning with the Elixir

The triumphant hero returns to the ordinary world bearing the object of the quest, as well as some secondary prize. Common secondary prizes are treasure, love, freedom, wisdom, or knowledge. The hero is changed by their experience and usually doesn't quite fit in at home, so either changes their home to fit them, or lives apart. A failed hero is doomed to repeat the quest until they learn the lesson inherent in it.

As I said above, this plot map isn't the be-all and end-all for how narrative journeys must be structured. This is just an example, albeit one of the most popular in the male-centric European Western canon. Many other cultures have many different storytelling traditions and structures.

Having said all this, it makes a strong case for why culturebuilding is important. The home culture of your protagonist is where they start their story and, ultimately, it's where they return, changed. The juxtaposition of the protagonist in their home culture before their adventure, and then after it, highlights just how very much the character has transformed and grown during the narrative.

Let's use *The Lord of the Rings* books as an example. In the first novel of the trilogy[6], Frodo Baggins has grown up wealthy and privileged as the heir of his eccentric uncle Bilbo. The Shire is an agrarian paradise, where food and good cheer are valued. It is a very prosperous and privileged life, where, if he had stayed in the Shire, his greatest hardship may have been picking a spouse to carry on the vaunted Baggins name. But leave, Frodo does.

When he returns to the Shire, the culture of his hometown is unchanged (and in the film version[7], the Razing never happens, so the physical idyllic green world is also preserved), but Frodo himself is altered by his experience.

The dissonance between who he is, and who his fellow Hobbits think he ought to still be, is a contributing factor in his choice to seek solace in the Grey Havens at the end of the tale. While Frodo returns to the Shire, because of his ordeal, the culture of the Shire is no longer home *for Frodo.*

---

[6] Tolkien, J.R.R. *The Lord of the Rings: the Fellowship of the Ring*. (George Allen & Unwin, 1954).

[7] Jackson, Peter (dir.) *The Lord of the Rings: the Fellowship of the Ring*. (Newline Cinema, 2001).

The Hero's Journey Narrative Cycle[8]

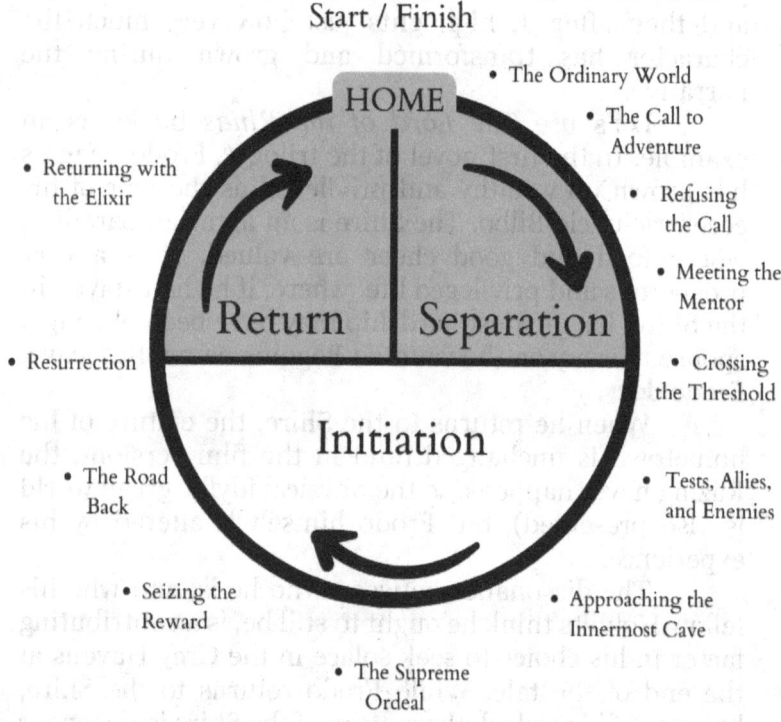

---
[8] Chart adapted from:
Campbell, Joseph. *The Hero with a Thousand Faces.* (Pantheon Books, 1968).

Hegemony and Unconscious Bias

From the Greek word translating as *supreme* or *supremacy*, a 'hegemon' was when a single city-state was given or took control of another city-state either through political means, military gains, or cultural/societal influence. Today, we would more closely associate the classical understanding of 'hegemony' with Colonialism, which is the subjugation and forced assimilation of one society by another.

However, when talking about 'hegemony' in sociological terms, though it's freighted with some connotation of control, we're focussing more on the aspect that asks us to confront the taught belief that a cultural construct is naturally occurring, and therefore without bias.

Let me break that down for you.

Beliefs, habits, traditions, and biases (both conscious and unconscious) are *taught* behaviour. As children, we are all educated in the way our society works both explicitly by our teachers and parents, and implicitly by what we witness and reason out about what is happening around us.

An explicit lesson may come from a child being scolded for taking a toy out of another child's hands; the explicit lesson is that we don't take things that belong to others. An implicit lesson may come from watching another parent guide their child to what they consider a 'gender appropriate' toy. Though no one said out loud "cars are for boys, dolls are for girls", a young boy steered away from a doll imparts the implicit lesson, however consciously acknowledged, to both that boy-child and any children watching the interaction, that nurturing-play is not supposed to be for boys.

When an implicit lesson is reinforced over and over by other instances and circumstances, the child comes to accept it as a natural truth of the world. *Even though*, as we all know, there is nothing inherently gendered about caring for, or loving our offspring, continued implicit and explicit education turns it into an unconscious bias. As an adult, the child may strongly and erroneously believe that men are incapable of nurturing children.

This learned opinion becomes unconsciously enshrined as a 'law of nature', simply because the society they were nurtured and educated in tells them it is true.

In this situation it is the *thought* that is hegemonic. That is, the 'supreme' thing that is controlling a person in a society is not an outside force, like a conquering nation, but an inside force: the *culture* itself.

We believe a thing is true, and inherent, and natural, because (unbeknownst to us), we have been *taught* to believe that this thing is true, inherent, and natural.

Why does this matter as a writer?

Because you are creating a culture, you're probably going to want to fill it with cultural biases that will inform the choices, behaviours, and habits of your characters.

For example, imagine a culture where pacifism is a societal priority and people have been raised to believe that it is abhorrently wrong and unnatural for one person to assault another. If a character raised in that culture is then confronted with a situation where they have to commit physical violence to save their own life, the character will probably hesitate, even if only for a moment, before doing so. And in the aftermath of the violence, they will likely feel guilty, disgusted, and angry with themselves. This gives the writer a *fantastic* opportunity for a heartfelt, deep character moment that creates friction and movement in the plot.

But it's also important, when creating a new culture, to examine our *own* internal unconscious biases. New cultures are blank slates, so it is important to examine which of our own norms, traditions, and taboos we are importing, and imposing on the world we create. Be cautious of your own knee-jerk response to say "it's just the way it is", or "it's always been like that", or "this is what it was like in the past," when investigating the whys and hows of the culture you're inventing. Chances are, what you think is normal and natural is actually learned, and therefore might not need to be included.

To further demonstrate this, let's take a quick look at a case study that demonstrates this unconscious bias: the belief that "red means stop".

Red Means Stop

Red is a warning colour. Because of its wavelength, red is one of the most visible colours to the human eye at night[9]. It catches our attention easily and quickly, and we can see it from further away than any of the other colours. As the opposite colour to green on the colour wheel, it contrasts sharply with vegetation. Cultures all over the world have words for Black, White, and Red, sometimes even if they don't have words for other colours. (Some theories suggest that it took the Greeks some time to come up with a word for 'blue', hence Homer's "wine-dark sea".)[10]

Red is also the colour of blood, of fire, and of many poisonous creatures and plants. Red flowers attract pollinators. Red prey can be spotted against green-and-brown foliage (and warn those that may try to eat them that it's a bad idea), and red predators can be seen against a blue sky. Everything in the natural world tells us that red things deserve our immediate attention to avoid danger, or to mitigate harm, or to help someone who has been hurt, or entices us to interact with a plant in order to help it scatter pollen or seeds by picking it and / or eating it.

So naturally, when it comes to creating warning signs, humans tend to gravitate towards making them red. When red appears on modern flags used by sailing

---

[9] "Red". *Wikipedia.org*. <https://en.wikipedia.org/wiki/Red> Accessed 10/26/2022.

[10] "*Wine-Dark Sea (Homer)*". *Wikipedia.org*. <https://en.wikipedia.org/wiki/Wine-dark_sea_(Homer)> Accessed: 10/29/2022.

vessels, the meaning of that particular flag generally indicates a warning to stay away because of a danger (hauling live ammunition, man overboard, etc.) or a plea for assistance (we need a medic, we require a tug, etc.)[11]

But why, specifically, do traffic lights include the colour red? Well, it's because of trains.

As trains got faster and more complex, signals relayed to the conductor had to be visible from further and further away, including at night. From hand signals by a blockman officer, to wooden semaphore signals on hinged arms, lamps were eventually introduced in the latter half of the 1800s to communicate messages to the drivers.[12]

At first, the lanterns consisted of a simple white lens, with a second white lens covered by a transparent red cap.

Apocryphal legend states that a major railway accident occurred somewhere in the late 1800s or early 1900s, which saw one of the red lenses pop off a lamp. As the conductor saw two white lights, indicating that they should continue, they went ahead and crashed head-on with another train. Whether an accident of this nature really did occur or not up for debate, but it was around this time that signalling methods were refined, and a green lens was added to the second lamp[13]. Now neither of the lights were white, so if a lens popped off, a white light would act as a warning that there was a mechanical issue. Green and Red are contrasting values on the colour wheel, making it easy to differentiate between the two lamps.

---

[11]Edwards, Chris. "The Meanings of Boat Flags". *Vispronet.com*. 05/10/2018. <https://www.vispronet.com/blog/meanings-boat-flags/>
Accessed: 06/23/2022.

[12]"Railway Signalling". "*Wikipedia.org*.
<https://en.wikipedia.org/wiki/Railway_signalling>
Accessed: 08/08/2022.

[13] Solomon, Brian. *Railroad Signalling*. (Voyager Press, 2003).

And so, Green Means Go and Red Means Stop became the rule wherever trains and this control system spread. Eventually the amber light was added to indicate that trains should prepare to stop soon, in order to give the massive machines time to begin slowing down before a stoppage was ordered.

This system of signaling was devised in the United Kingdom, and was implemented everywhere the British colonized and established railroads. Thus, the concept of Red Means Stop travelled to every continent and corner of the world.

When automobiles became more commonplace, a system of organization was required for drivers. The first electric traffic signal was installed in Cleveland in 1914, and was designed by James Hoge. He adopted the Green and Red signals from trains, as many people were already familiar with their cultural significance. The tricolour traffic signal we use today first appeared in 1920 in Detroit, designed by police officer William Potts[14].

Through both Colonization and Entertainment Media, this system of organizing traffic spread across the world, and you can now find the tricoloured traffic lights pretty much everywhere you find automobiles.

Now, think about a character from a world without trains, and signalmen, and traffic lights.

Would King Arthur know how to read the stoplights if he were suddenly to appear in Times Square? Probably not. However, Arthur would likely be clever enough to figure out how to read the traffic lights by watching the patterns of traffic movement, and the reactions of the people around him.

Out of context, "red means stop" on a tricolour traffic light may be baffling to King Arthur. But in context, at a street corner, he could quickly pick up the concept by observing fellow pedestrians. And being human, King

---

[14] "The strange history of the humble traffic light". *Driving.ca*. 04/10/2014<https://driving.ca/local-content/maritimes/traffic-lights-loved-and-hated> Accessed: 06/23/2022.

Arthur would likely already be familiar with red as a danger signal.

But what about an alien from another planet, where the chemical composition of the atmosphere scatters the light in a different way, and red isn't the most noticeable colour? Would they be familiar with the colour red at all? What would be the attention-grabbing colour on their homeworld? What would it mean if they were confronted with traffic lights here on Earth?

What kind of narrative friction would this change cause, especially to other characters who still operate with the internal bias of "red means stop"? How can you turn that into a narrative or character moment? What other "this is just the way things are" biases can you play with to develop a rich and unique culture?

Culturebuilding and Character

Culture is conveyed *through* character.

In the same way that you may devise a map to illustrate where your character came from, where they travel on their adventures, and what sights they see along the way, so too should you devise a culture for them to have grown up in and take along with them.

Maps show the reader where the character came from physically. A culture shows the reader where the character came from mentally and emotionally. While the former is a visual representation, the latter is harder to put on the page, but I would argue is far more important.

Culture informs every choice your character is going to make. Every action. Every preference. Every opinion.

It bubbles up through the dialogue of your character, in the idioms and beliefs, in the values they hold, the way they react to certain situations, and the way other characters react and interact with them.

So creating a culture for your character to originate from is important. It will help shape the character themselves, but also present the building blocks of conflict for the plot, especially if the values of their home culture are discordant with their later choices and desires.

Creating a setting for your story to exist in is important, but people are influenced equally by both nature and nurture. As we discussed earlier, *where* they grow up informs their habits, preferences, and biases. But so does *how* they grow up.

So, what does that mean? This means that, while you are world-building, you also have to character-build– you need to focus on one person, or a group of people, and tell the story about *them* and not about the world itself.

How do you do that? Some people find it easier to start with the character and build the world based on what you need that character to be like. Some people find it easier to build the world and then pluck one of the people out of their world to focus on.

There is no right and wrong way to do it, but don't *forget* to do it. The character is the one that the story is about, not the world.

Remember, stories are about *people*, not *places*. No matter how awesome the world, and the culture you build is, these things are all just the support mechanism through which you relate the tragedies and triumphs of the people that populate your tale.

In telling the story of a character, you are automatically telling the story of the world they live in. If it is a world rich in tradition, stories, and understanding, then you can learn about the world at large by spending time in your character's smaller world: macrocosm via microcosm.

Who a person is and what they want are very much embedded in the hegemony of the culture in which they were raised. That means, you, as the writer, should probably have some idea of that culture not only on a grand worldbuilding scale, but how it directly affected the growth and values of your character. Yes, know the mechanics and the principals of the world at large, but also those of the neighbourhood that your character grew up in.

I find that when a writer has considered all of this, it shines through on the page, and the characters are more compelling, more in-depth, and more interesting to spend time with. Think of your favourite characters, and then think of what you know of their childhoods, their parents, the food they prefer and the entertainment they like. This makes them accessible, because we all have preferences and things we fear and like, too. This makes for an attractive character that people want to spend time with (even if they're an anti-hero), and with whom the reader grows comfortable.

Then it's easy to want to invest in a couple hundred pages worth of reading about this character, and their journey.

Above all, don't infodump. It is the story that is paramount when writing a novel, not the world. No matter how cool a thing you invented for your world may be, if it doesn't serve the story, don't waste pages describing it.

Think of it this way: good world / culture-building serves the plot. If something has to stop—some action, some conversation, some journey—so that someone has to explain something (even if that someone is you, the narrator / writer) then it is probably not necessary and can be cut. You can tell us that information, but find an engaging, active way to do so that keeps the story rolling.

I believe my audience is intelligent enough to infer the latter without beating them around the head with the facts.

To close, let me sum up:

Don't write a textbook. Write a novel about a person and let that person's life give all the clues about their culture the reader needs to understand the world in which they live, and the place they're coming from in a physical, mental, and emotional sense.

Culturebuilding and Storytelling

Here are a few great examples of how culturebuilding informs character and story.

WORLDBUILDING THROUGH CULTURE

As you read them, think about the opening of your story. How much culturebuilding can you fit into the first few paragraphs, and how subtly can you do so? How early can you sow the seeds of understanding, and foreshadow the revelations that are in later chapters?

Most importantly, how can you set your characters, your story, and your readers up for success and mutual understanding?

The Hobbit by J.R.R. Tolkien[15]

In a hole in the ground there lived a hobbit. Not a nasty, dirty, wet hole filled with the ends of worms and an oozy smell, nor yet a dry, bare, sandy hole with nothing in it to sit down or to eat: it was a hobbit-hole, and that means comfort.

What have we learned? That our protagonist is a hobbit. We don't know what hobbits are yet, but they live underground and they like comfort, and probably, based on what was said about the sandy holes, plush furniture and good meals. Readers can also infer, because I assume he's going to be the protagonist, this hobbit is human-esque, as readers prefer to read about creatures that resemble themselves.

So the World: Some sort of fantasy land, with creatures that we don't know, but who greatly resemble us in that they want comfort, safety, and good meals. We'll be with a protagonist who seems a lot like us, and thus easy to empathize with.

---

[15] Tolkien, J.R.R. *The Hobbit: Or, There and Back Again*. (George Allen & Unwin, 1937).

J.M. FREY

Do Androids Dream of Electric Sheep by Philip K. Dick[16]

A merry little surge of electricity piped by automatic alarm from the mood organ beside his bed awakened Rick Deckard. -Surprised—it always surprised him to find himself awake without prior notice—-he rose from the bed, stood up in his multicolored pajamas, and stretched. Now, in her bed, his wife Iran opened her gray, unmerry eyes, blinked, then groaned and shut her eyes again.

"You set your Penfield too weak," he said to her. "I'll reset it and you'll be awake and—-"
"Keep your hand off my settings." Her voice held bitter sharpness. "I don't want to be awake."
He seated himself beside her, bent over her, and explained softly. "If you set the surge up high enough, you'll be glad you're awake; that's the whole point. At setting C it overcomes the threshold barring consciousness, as it does for me." Friendlily, because he felt well--disposed toward the world—-his setting had been at D—-he patted her bare, pale shoulder.
"Get your crude cop's hand away," Iran said.
"I'm not a cop." He felt irritable, now, although he hadn't dialed for it.
"You're worse," his wife said, her eyes still shut. "You're a murderer hired by the cops."
"I've never killed a human being in my life." His irritability had risen now; had become outright hostility.
Iran said, "Just those poor andys."

What have we learned? Our protagonist is some sort of hunter who kills something called an "andy", which is not human. Despite this, his wife feels sympathy for them. The protagonist is married, and lives in a world with technology that allows you to control moods.

---

[16]Dick, Philip K. *Do Androids Dream of Electric Sheep* (Doubleday, 1968).

So the World: Science Fiction, with a level of bio-hacking technology in a domestic setting that conveys that tech and humanity is going to be a big part of the story. It also introduces a cop / bounty hunter character, which makes the reader think they may be in for a noir or detective novel set in a sci-fi world.

The Bogart by Susan Cooper[17]

> *The little boat crept closer, over the grey-green water of the loch. Tommy could hear the slow creaking of the oarlocks, and see the white hair of the lean old man bent over the oars. His father said the MacDevon was one hundred years old, but Tommy had never had the courage to ask if it were true. The MacDevon was a clan chief, the last of his line, and you didn't ask a clan chief a question like that.*
>
> *"Good Day, Mr. MacDevon." He caught the bow of the dinghy as it crunched into the small stones of the beach. This was a weekly ritual: the old man's shopping trip from the island of Castle Keep.*

What have we learned? That there is an old man who lives in a castle on an island in a loch; we are probably in Scotland, and that there is a young boy who helps the old man. We know that it must be closer to modern times, if the clan has died out and The MacDevon is the last of his line. We also know that the old man mustn't be wealthy, because he only owns an old dinghy that he has to row himself, and he has no one to send on his shopping errands.

So the World: Run down castle in modern Scotland where the clan chief is old but respected by the locals, and is possibly thought of as a quaint relic. We know this is a fantastical novel by the title, so we assume this bogart will be in the castle we've just been introduced to.

---

[17] Cooper, Susan. *The Bogart*. (MacMillan, 1993).

FINDING YOUR STARTING POINT

There are many different ways to take your first steps into the culture you're creating. Some people like to work on a story from the macro-to-micro level (the big picture things to the nitty gritty things), and others like to do it vice versa. There's no right way to start a story, or to start world / culturebuilding.

The point of this workbook is to help you take the nebulous big-picture macro-sized sort of setting problem-solving and / or nitty-gritty micro-sized concepts, and turn it all into a fully detailed set of notes that will allow you to tell a story in a believable, rich, and fascinating world. The workbook will help you get all the details on the page and out of your head, so you can stand back and look at the patterns and connections that they make when all woven together, and make them *deliberate*.

If you know the central tenants or general shape of the culture you intend to build, feel free to skip right to the next chapter, if you want. If you're still unsure, or if you want a little more help figuring it out, read on.

Culture-led Starting Point

If you have an idea of the world you want to create, but not the kind of people that you're going to make to populate it yet, then you're probably going to want to start from a cultural view point. In that case, give the general geography, climate, and location of your culture some thought. From there, consider how that would influence the folks who would settle there, and then (and this is the hard part) seize on a single object / concept / story / food source / major export, etc. that can serve as the central focal point of the intellectual and creative energies of the culture. That is, what is the one *nugget* of something that you can build a whole culture around?

If it's a sea-faring culture, what's the main *idea* of the culture? "Sea-faring" is a broad descriptor, and as we know from our world, sea-faring can mean many different things to many different people—just think about the culture of the Polynesian Island Samoa in 1722, and that of the Dutch explorers who first landed there that same year. Both cultures relied on the stars for navigation, but in different ways. Both had ports and trade routes between their own settlements, but also between other nations and islands. Yet in terms of cuisine, beliefs, fashion, storytelling, music, etc. we wouldn't consider the two cultures very similar at all. Yet both are 'sea-faring,' coastal cultures.

For your fictional culture, try to hone in on something specific that makes your culture unique, a signifier or marker of the culture. Then blow it outward by seeing how you can parlay it into things like fashion, food, and fun.

Perhaps for a fantasy novel, the nugget may be 'sea monsters'. In this fictional coastal, sea-faring culture, do they revere or revile sea monsters? Are sea monsters real, are they real but hidden, or are they only imaginary? Do the villagers *know* that monsters are real, or imaginary? In what way are sea monsters centred in the culture / fashion / architecture / stories / music / cuisine / of the fictional culture? Are they captured and processed for food and clothing, or are they pets? Are they mindless beasts to be avoided at all cost, or are they sentient and a part of society?

Of course it doesn't have to be something quite so tangible. I, personally, like to think up interesting and creative ways for the characters to cuss. Generally speaking, in contemporary languages curse words are usually a) blaspheming against a deity / religion / organization or higher power, be they tangible or governmental, b) crassly sexual, c) a specific regional or cultural reference or idiom, d) all of the above.

I tend to gravitate to version A, as it gives me the most room to construct logic puzzles that help define a culture. If you know what someone in a society curses or blasphemes, then you know what they hold holy (whether spiritually, religiously, or on an agnostic social level). If you know what they venerate, then you know what they aspire to become or hold dear. If you know their aspirations, then you know their ideals. If you know their ideals, then you know what the whole of the society is centered around and strives for.

That is a *great* place to start building a culture.

Let's think about another example, this time a sci-fi society that exists in a self-contained spaceship. Let's say it's a small craft that needs to be rigorously maintained, and kept hygienic. Everyone onboard has rigidly set chore schedules. The craft is too small and the people too valuable to lose anyone to illness or accidents, and especially not to violence. Peace and cleanliness may be your nuggets, as these are the highest ideals of the ship—the kernel of an idea for the culture, that you will then explode outwards like popcorn.

So think about how that would translate into everyday idioms, into metaphors and poetic language, and into cuss words. This allows for an especially unique and isolated culture if this tale takes place on an intergenerational ship, and your characters are several lifetimes removed from their home planet, with no emotional or nostalgic attachment to the culture their ancestors left behind. Imagine the interesting ways of speaking that would evolve—and the interesting ways of conflict management, ensuring the next generation thrives, and the notions of responsibility to an outside power (in this case, the mission to make it to a new planet with the society intact and functioning), and what kind of social conditioning and propaganda that would require to maintain. Imagine how rigorously leaders would need to enforce it, and how seriously they would need to punish or make examples of outliers, for the good of the survival of the rest.

Once you have the nugget chosen and an outline of the culture sketched out, you can start zeroing in on a particular protagonist, or group of characters, who will both embody and navigate within the culture.

Or, perhaps you prefer to start with people first.

Character-led Starting Point

As I said in a previous chapter, all the worldbuilding in the world won't turn your idea into a story. You need a character or two to follow to do that, and a reason we're following that particular character.

What kind of story do you want to tell? A high-fantasy quest narrative? An emotional literary fiction tale about love and loss? A science fiction action adventure? What sort of person does your protagonist have to be to fit that kind of story? What occupation or talent do they need to have in order to be active in the plot? Or, more interestingly, how could you work with a character who *doesn't* fit in, or isn't usually featured, in this kind of story?

Some more things to mull over:

- What gender is this character?
- What biological sex?
- What age?
- What class?
- What ethnicity?
- What stage of their life are they in, and does your fictional culture measure life-stages the same way your real-life one does?
- What is it that the character wants, and how is the character going to work to get it?
- Who or what is going to get in their way and how will they deal with being denied what they want? How will they overcome this obstacle?

- What do they fear most, above all else, and what would happen if they were to be forced to endure the thing they fear?
- Why do they fear that thing? What's the socio-economic reason, the culture-based reason, rather than the personal-backstory-trauma reason?
- Why does this person need to be your protagonist, and not say, their sibling, or neighbour, or oppressor, or slave, or pet?
- How close are they to their immediate family, what is their relationship with them like, and how obligated to that relationship are they? How will that relationship influence the decisions that your protagonist makes in later moments of crisis?
- How integrated in their community is your protagonist? How obligated to that community do they feel, and how will that relationship influence the decisions that your protagonist makes in later moments of crisis?

Basically: *who* is this person, and *why* them?

These are a lot of questions, I know. You don't have to answer them now—there's actually space set aside for all that later in the workbook. But I want you to start *thinking* about them now, because everything you do in terms of worldbuilding will be framed and disseminated to the reader through the viewpoint and experiences of your protagonist.

In answering these questions, you'll begin to world-build alongside this; to know why your character fears X instead of Y, you'll need to decide what that means in the scope of their culture and upbringing. You can get at the culture by building it up around the character, bit by bit.

If culture-led starting points are like a kernel of popcorn, then character-led starting points are like a sand castle, piled bucketful by bucketful around the stick or pile of rocks that is your protagonist, until you can shape and finesse the final outward edifice.

Culture and Misunderstanding

Another great way to worldbuild via character is by allowing your protagonist to experience things they *don't* understand, or aren't familiar with. Much of a protagonist's beliefs and way of life can be exposed and explained to the reader in context, by sticking them in a place where those same beliefs and way of life don't match those of the people around them.

How they react to new experiences, ideologies, or manners tells the reader a lot about their home culture, and how they were raised.

What confuses your protagonist? What offends them? What shocks or startles them? What happens that makes them think, "Oh, that's a much better way of doing it than the way my people do it!" What new food delights them, and which disgusts them? What fashion seems indecent, and what seems prudish?

Dropping your protagonist in a cultural situation that's unfamiliar to them also provides the opportunity to give the reader a better understanding of your protagonist's personal characteristics. Do they react to new things with delight, or fear, or anger? Does change thrill or scare them? What does that tell your reader about the kind of person they are, and how they'll react to later, bigger misunderstandings or changes? Can you use these sorts of reactions to convey character growth, by showing your character reacting one way the first time, and a different way later?

A protagonist's habits and preferences can fill out the world as you go. Use what you've decided about their world to explain why they do some of the things they do, and how those cultural differences may act as sources of conflict or revelation between the protagonist and other characters.

Starting on Page One

However you choose to get into your world, you're going to find that you're going to have to re-think, revise, and revisit your decisions and assumptions many times over as you work through this book. *And* as you work through writing the first draft of your project.

That's okay. That's what creating is: tweaking, jiggling, editing, re-doing, ripping apart, building back up, and finessing. Nothing is perfect in the first draft, and nothing is meant to be.

But before you can edit, you have to write. And before you can write, you have to invent.

So let's start.

THE BIG QUESTIONS

There are the four things that humans need to not only survive, but thrive: Food, Shelter, Protection, and a way to Share Information. Historically, culture explodes when a society is thriving, when the people are well-rested, well-fed, and well-loved. Oral storytelling, performance, and music-making can happen anywhere and everywhere, but when people are safe and happy, with idle hours and strong communities (not necessarily settled in one place, because rich nomadic cultures exist) you then find a wealth of theatre, textile, and visual art.

Safety and security means leisure time, and leisure time means culture. So before we get to the fun stuff, let's map out the basics that will allow your culture to thrive.

The Big Four

In this next section, we're going to take a broad look at the four things I listed above.

I assume that by now you've taken some time to mull over what sort of fictional culture you're looking to build, and what your starting point will be. Now it's time to uncap that pen, or sharpen that pencil, and start scribbling in this workbook.

Ready?

Here we go.

Food and Drink

What people eat, how they gain access to food and water, and how much of their day is taken up with hunting or gathering, preparing, cooking, and consuming food has an effect on how much leftover time they have for leisure activities and cultural pursuits. When people have the time to prepare food as more than just sustenance, innovation and culinary art flourish.

Cuisine is an expression of culture.

Think of the basics of where food would have first been available, in this world. What was immediately edible when people first settled the area, like berries and fruit? What required a little preparation or exertion, like hunting game or fish? What required a far more complicated process and specialty tools, like farming wheat, milling it, and making it into bread? Then think about how long the people have been in this spot, what short cuts or innovations they may have created. How technologically advanced is society, and what does that mean in terms of kitchen gadgets and conveniences?

Who is involved in the production of food (the farming, fishing, packaging, processing, sale)? How far removed from the process is your protagonist (do they live on the farm and only eat what they grow, or do they only buy pre-packaged and processed goods?)

Broadly, what does your protagonist consume?

Shelter and Architecture

The climate of where someone lives will dictate where, why, and how their shelters are constructed. A building designed to keep out significant amounts of rain differs from the construction of a building designed to stay cool on a sweltering afternoon. Innovations in technology and building material availability, and environmental considerations, will change shelter-design, evolving over time. Community identity, nostalgia, and tradition will create a distinct look and way of building for that society.

Architecture is an expression of culture.

The way your society uses buildings will also dictate how they're constructed. Are they single-purpose, like a school, a military base, a shopping mall? Or are businesses run out of homes, do people sleep in the market, is the throne room also a billet for travellers?

How old are the buildings / structures they live in? Do people inherit or live in other people's homes, or is a building / structure torn down or remade with each new inhabitant?

Who creates these structures, and how far removed from the process is your protagonist? Did your protagonist make their own, did someone else make it for them, were they assigned it, or is it long-since inherited from generations past?

Broadly, where does your protagonist live, and how do they stay out of the elements?

_____
_____
_____
_____
_____
_____
_____
_____

Clothing and Textiles

Like shelter, clothing exists to protect humanity's naked, furless and scale-less flesh from injury. It helps us to do specific jobs without getting hurt, and survive in climates that would otherwise kill us. Think back to the beginning of your society's establishment—whether on a generational starship or a coastal fantasy town, or something else—and think about what elements and dangers people would have needed to protect themselves from. Was it deep snow? Lashing rains? Biting insects? The void of space? What jobs do they do—fishing, mecha repairs, soldiering, personal care—and what clothing will protect them, keep them from harm, and make their jobs easier to do?

Fashion is an expression of culture.

How are spiritual beliefs, folklore, or religion reflected in what they wear, and how they wear it? How do major cultural influences like wars, the monarchy, celebrities, notions of sexiness or modesty, or international trade affect the quantity of fabric available, the parts of the body left exposed, the quality of tailoring, and the cycle of trends?

How far removed from the origins of a particular traditional mode of dress is your protagonist? How far from the production of textiles and clothing are they? Do they dress in a uniform daily, or do they make their own clothes? Do they have multiple outfits to choose from, or just a few sets?

Broadly, what sorts of things does your protagonist wear?

Communication and Information

Sharing information that will keep the community safe and allow it to thrive is not a uniquely human trait, but humans do it in an infinite variety. Like bees dancing to communicate the location of pollen caches, humans tell one another about the locations of safe water, or poisonous berries to avoid. We advertise goods, services, and innovations. We trade news of wars and weather, warn one another away from dangerous places like sinkholes and the path of a lava flow, and send cards to express joy on happy milestone occasions.

As societies with different languages begin to interact, ways of communicating vital information have increasingly moved towards pictograms: the skull-and-crossbones to denote something poisonous or dangerous, emojis, or directional signals like arrows.

And of course, we tell stories. Stories to teach, stories to delight, stories to warn, stories to grieve.

Entertainment is an expression of culture.

How close to the source of news is your protagonist? Where do they get theirs? How much do they know of the wider world, and is the information that reaches them biased in any way? How do they entertain themselves, or those around them? How are they educated?

Broadly, how does your protagonist receive and share information that is considered necessary?

WORLDBUILDING THROUGH CULTURE

FOOD & DRINK

What is their staple grain / food product?

What sort of climate do they live in and what kind of agriculture does that allow them to have?

Do they eat meat? Do they raise it? Hunt it? Fish for it?

Is food eaten cooked or raw?

Do they grow and process their own food?

Are they able to grow / gather / hunt for enough food for themselves, or do they need supplemental food?

Where do they buy supplementary food, and does it cost a lot? Do they trade for it? Do they barter?

Are there specialists like butchers or millers? How are they treated in society?

Are their services free or provided by the government, or are they wildly expensive?

Are there foods that are imported or exported?

Are exotic / difficult to grow or obtain foods expensive and a sign of largesse, or wastefulness?

What was your protagonist's childhood treat?

What food does your protagonist consider necessary and healthy, but yucky?

What is served for special occasions?

What happens to food waste? Is there any?

Does food have a religious connotation or ritual?

Is there a concept of a national or regional cuisine?

What food product, type of cuisine, or singular dish is your society's best known?

Can people have food allergies, and how widely known are they? Are they accommodated or ignored?

Do certain sects, classes, or segments of society eat foods prepared a certain way, or only have access to certain food products?

WORLDBUILDING THROUGH CULTURE

How is food distributed to those who can't afford to buy it? Are they fed at all? Are they fed *well*?

Is the water safe to drink? If not, what do they drink instead?

What do they do in times of famine and drought? Are they prepared in advance? Has this happened before?

How do they make food last longer?

Do they make and/or consume alcohol or hallucinogens? When and how? Recreationally or ritually?

Is food shared? Communal cooking and eating? Family-only? Solo-only? Who cooks?

Is all food delivered daily? What's the logistics system for that? Does everyone get the same meal?

Are there picky eaters? Is it normal or considered extremely rude to not like some foods?

What is considered good / bad table manners?

Are there cookbooks and recipes? Do they get shared or passed around?

Are there restaurants? Take-away meals?

What do they eat on the go? *Do* they eat while travelling?

Is eating in public normal, or weird, or rude?

Is being a chef / cook a profession? An art?

Is the kitchen a separate room of the domicile?

How do they heat and cook their food? A hearth? A stove? A fancy sci-fi microwave?

What do they drink, besides water?

How does a ready supply of fresh water get into the house?

Do they flavour water with tea, fruit, ground beans?

Do they drink the milk of other mammals?

What do they ferment drinks?

Do they have the ability to carbonize drinks?

Are certain kinds of drinks only for a certain segment of the population (age / class / ethnicity / religion /etc.)?

Is the rainwater safe to drink?

Is the groundwater safe to drink?

CLOTHING & TEXTILES

What materials are most clothes made of?

Where do they obtain these materials?

How is raw cloth made?

How are clothes dyed?

Can you buy raw cloth easily? Dyes? Sewing materials?

Are fabrics imported or exported? Why? What techniques do other cultures use that your culture has no knowledge or experience in?

Who does the dying? Cutting? Sewing? Tailoring?

Are clothes thrown away when they tear or stain? Or are they repaired?

Do people wear hand-me-downs or remake old clothes?

Who is responsible for laundering clothes, and how often are they cleaned?

Is making / designing clothing a profession? An art form?

What do the people around your protagonist wear, and what do the people below and above the protagonist in class / station / career / etc. wear? Can you tell from a glance who is who?

What do they wear lounging around at home?

What do they wear to work? Is it practical or ornamental or symbolic? Is it just something they wear to blend in?

What do they wear at their most fancy?

Are there some colours or fabrics that certain people cannot or do not wear? Why?

How much does it cost to buy premade clothing? To make your own? What's more expensive, bespoke or ready-made?

What part of the body is it considered lewd not to cover?

What part of the body does everyone display?

Is there a concept of fashion, high fashion, or trends?

Who follows trends, and why?

Who wears uniforms, and why?

Do your people send secret messages with how and when they wear certain clothes or accessories?

Do people have many outfits, or just a few they reuse?

Who makes the footwear? How do people obtain it?

Are any sorts of ceremonial clothes retained, or considered family heirlooms, or reworn?

Is there specialized clothing for specialized occupations that have become trendy (like cableknit sweaters?)

CLIMATE & SHELTER

Is your culture stationary or nomadic? Both?

How long are the seasons and how does this affect how much indoor/outdoor living time they may have?

What percentage of their "living space" is outdoors?

What elements are they protecting themselves from?

What materials are available in the immediate area to make a rudimentary shelter out of?

Which are imported or manufactured elsewhere? How are they transported to the building site?

What ingenious architectural quirks have they invented to deal with their particular climate challenges?

Is their place of business separate from their home?

Is their place of worship separate from their home?

How close are homes to each other, to work, to schools, to shopping centers, etc.? How is the community *organized*? Is it?

WORLDBUILDING THROUGH CULTURE

Are there separate rooms for separate purposes?

What furniture is considered vital and which is frivolous?

Is there indoor plumbing?

Is bathing private or communal? What are the rituals of bathing, and how often do they do so?

What is the level of privacy between family members?

Between visitors and the family?

Do people visit each other's dwellings?

Can people lose their homes? What happens to the unhoused?

How does a new family (newlyweds, the homeless, refugees and immigrants, etc.) get a house?

Is there special space set aside for entertainment, and is it in the house, or is it communal (pubs, assembly halls, etc.)

NEWS & INFORMATION

Is there a written language? If yes, who can learn it and where do they learn? If no, why not?

Is there more than a single verbal language/tongue? Who can learn multiple ones? Why would they? Why wouldn't they?

Is there a physical or voiceless language or way of communicating? (gestures like nodding, sucking teeth when it's impolite to say 'no', a fully developed sign language, etc.)

How are ancestral knowledge or stories passed from one generation to another?

How is skill / trade / occupational information passed between people (farming techniques, recipes, etc.)

How are children educated, and on what topics?

How is general information disseminated? (Newspaper, letters and postal system, computers, pigeon?)

How is *emergency* information disseminated?

Is there a concept of lying?

WORLDBUILDING THROUGH CULTURE

Are lies punished?

Do they have fictional stories, fairy tales, morality plays, myths and legends, etc.?

What sorts of stories do they tell to explain the natural workings of the world? Science or myth?

Are people employed as journalists or truth-seekers?

Are people employed as storytellers or fiction writers?

Is there culturally shared and often performed song cycles / epic poems or eddas / canon of plays, etc.

Are storytellers celebrated? Is it a special skill or occupation? Or is it just fancy lying?

How is information stored, and recalled? (Libraries, archives, professional memoirists, etc.)

Where do you go, if you want to learn or find information?

Is some knowledge secret or classified? Can regular folk gain access to it?

What are the biases (unconscious or conscious / propaganda-like) of the people creating and distributing the news and information?

Do the people in charge use propaganda to sway / bolster / incentivise / terrorize the public?

Who controls the propaganda? For what purpose?

Is there counter-propaganda?

How do people spread information that the leaders or governments *don't* want shared?

How do people ensure that the truth is being told in vital moments, such as in court or on resumes?

What oaths or promises do people make when pledging themselves or their support to a cause?

What is the punishment for oathbreakers?

Can children be held accountable for spreading misinformation? How are their lies or tall tales handled?

THE SMALL QUESTIONS

Now that you've got the four foundational cornerstones and the framework of your culture situated, we can start to investigate deeper details. What follows here is a very long list of questions. It's not expected that you will know the answer to each right away as soon as you get to the section. It's alright to skip questions and come back to them later, or to change your mind and re-answer them.

Culturebuilding, like storytelling, is a process of evolution, of revision, of edits, and of going back in to tweak. Or, as author Neil Gaiman[18] says:

Replying to @DanaSchwartzzz

Write down everything that happens in the story, and then in your second draft make it look like you knew what you were doing all along.

4:17 PM · Jan 30, 2018 · TweetDeck

It's okay to really *work* this workbook. The point is not to get a perfectly concise and logical culture right away. There are no gold stars for speed here. Cultures, like the writing process, can be messy, contradictory, illogical, frustrating, and unfair.

---

[18]Gaiman, Neil. Tweet. 01/30/2018. <https://twitter.com/neilhimself/status/958449061417439233?lang=en> Accessed 10/29/2022.

SYSTEMS OF GOVERNMENT

How is their society ruled or organized?

Who:

What:

Where:

When:

Why:

Precedent / Genesis:

Most Privileged:

Least Privileged:

WORLDBUILDING THROUGH CULTURE

Who makes the laws, and who enforces them?

Who:

What:

Where:

When:

Why:

Precedent / Genesis:

Most Privileged:

Least Privileged:

What is the process for laws to be decided? Updated? Overturned?

Who:

What:

Where:

When:

Why:

Precedent / Genesis:

Most Privileged:

Least Privileged:

WORLDBUILDING THROUGH CULTURE

Is the ruler / leader feared, or loved, and why? Does it matter?

Who:

What:

Where:

When:

Why:

Precedent / Genesis:

Most Privileged:

Least Privileged:

How is the one or ones who rule / govern addressed?
What is their reputation among common folk?

Who:

What:

Where:

When:

Why:

Precedent / Genesis:

Most Privileged:

Least Privileged:

WORLDBUILDING THROUGH CULTURE

Is there a revolution or a war happening, or on the horizon? Who is fighting it, and what are their aims?

Who:

What:

Where:

When:

Why:

Precedent / Genesis:

Most Privileged:

Least Privileged:

How do the people have a voice in what happens in government? Do all the people get the right to express their choice and opinions?

Who:

What:

Where:

When:

Why:

Precedent / Genesis:

Most Privileged:

Least Privileged:

WORLDBUILDING THROUGH CULTURE

What happens to those who break the laws regarding how the systems of governance are organized and upheld?

Who:

What:

Where:

When:

Why:

Precedent / Genesis:

Most Privileged:

Least Privileged:

What happens to those who violate voting rights, or push back against the divine right of kings, or destroy the sanctity of peaceful transitions of power?

Who:

What:

Where:

When:

Why:

Precedent / Genesis:

Most Privileged:

Least Privileged:

WORLDBUILDING THROUGH CULTURE

HUMAN RIGHTS

Who are considered "persons" under the law?

Who:

What:

Where:

When:

Why:

Precedent / Genesis:

Most Privileged:

Least Privileged:

Can these laws/views regarding 'personhood-ness' be changed? If so, how?

Who:

What:

Where:

When:

Why:

Precedent / Genesis:

Most Privileged:

Least Privileged:

WORLDBUILDING THROUGH CULTURE

Do prisoners, criminals, and outsiders have rights and protections? Are they still persons, or do they lose that status?

Who:

What:

Where:

When:

Why:

Precedent / Genesis:

Most Privileged:

Least Privileged:

Can people own / control other people?

Who:

What:

Where:

When:

Why:

Precedent / Genesis:

Most Privileged:

Least Privileged:

WORLDBUILDING THROUGH CULTURE

Is there institutionalized slavery? Is it well-known and visible, or underground and black-market? Do people approve or deride it?

Who:

What:

Where:

When:

Why:

Precedent / Genesis:

Most Privileged:

Least Privileged:

Are a specific group of people considered non-persons under the law / by tradition / by taboo?

Who:

What:

Where:

When:

Why:

Precedent / Genesis:

Most Privileged:

Least Privileged:

WORLDBUILDING THROUGH CULTURE

What does the law have to say about this versus what tradition has to say about slavery / non-persons?

Who:

What:

Where:

When:

Why:

Precedent / Genesis:

Most Privileged:

Least Privileged:

Can people become un-owned by another? By what method?

Who:

What:

Where:

When:

Why:

Precedent / Genesis:

Most Privileged:

Least Privileged:

WORLDBUILDING THROUGH CULTURE

Can children become emancipated? By what method?

Who:

What:

Where:

When:

Why:

Precedent / Genesis:

Most Privileged:

Least Privileged:

PEOPLE WHO ARE NOT LIKE US

How does your culture define "Other"? By nation? Language? Skin tone? Religion? etc.

Who:

What:

Where:

When:

Why:

Precedent / Genesis:

Most Privileged:

Least Privileged:

WORLDBUILDING THROUGH CULTURE

Does your culture trade / speak / war with another culture?

Who:

What:

Where:

When:

Why:

Precedent / Genesis:

Most Privileged:

Least Privileged:

Are people who are different from your protagonist to be trusted, or distrusted, simply by virtue of their difference?

Who:

What:

Where:

When:

Why:

Precedent / Genesis:

Most Privileged:

Least Privileged:

WORLDBUILDING THROUGH CULTURE

What happens when they meet strangers?

Who:

What:

Where:

When:

Why:

Precedent / Genesis:

Most Privileged:

Least Privileged:

Are there concepts of Race and Ethnicity? Racism? Colonialism?

Who:

What:

Where:

When:

Why:

Precedent / Genesis:

Most Privileged:

Least Privileged:

WORLDBUILDING THROUGH CULTURE

Do they even understand that Racism and Colonialism are bad, destructive things to practice?

Who:

What:

Where:

When:

Why:

Precedent / Genesis:

Most Privileged:

Least Privileged:

Would your main character help a stranger in need or pain? Would other people in their community?

Who:

What:

Where:

When:

Why:

Precedent / Genesis:

Most Privileged:

Least Privileged:

WORLDBUILDING THROUGH CULTURE

Are people who are "Other" considered 'people' at all? Legally? Spiritually?

Who:

What:

Where:

When:

Why:

Precedent / Genesis:

Most Privileged:

Least Privileged:

OPPRESSION & TYRANNY

Are your people oppressed?

Who:

What:

Where:

When:

Why:

Precedent / Genesis:

Most Privileged:

Least Privileged:

WORLDBUILDING THROUGH CULTURE

If they are oppressed, are they aware of it?

Who:

What:

Where:

When:

Why:

Precedent / Genesis:

Most Privileged:

Least Privileged:

Are those in power tyrannical? Do they rule through oppression and fear?

Who:

What:

Where:

When:

Why:

Precedent / Genesis:

Most Privileged:

Least Privileged:

WORLDBUILDING THROUGH CULTURE

Who are the least privileged, most oppressed, most agency-denied peoples in your world? Why are they so?

Who:

What:

Where:

When:

Why:

Precedent / Genesis:

Most Privileged:

Least Privileged:

Who are the most privileged, the least oppressed? Are they the ones doing the oppressing? Why are they where they are?

Who:

What:

Where:

When:

Why:

Precedent / Genesis:

Most Privileged:

Least Privileged:

WORLDBUILDING THROUGH CULTURE

Where are the class / race / religion / ethnic tensions as a result of these different levels of oppression?

Who:

What:

Where:

When:

Why:

Precedent / Genesis:

Most Privileged:

Least Privileged:

Are the people of your culture hunted by anyone? Are your people livestock themselves? Or outcasts?

Who:

What:

Where:

When:

Why:

Precedent / Genesis:

Most Privileged:

Least Privileged:

WORLDBUILDING THROUGH CULTURE

WAR & VIOLENCE

Is violence an acceptable recourse for any reason?

Who:

What:

Where:

When:

Why:

Precedent / Genesis:

Most Privileged:

Least Privileged:

Is violence considered taboo, or animalistic, or below them?

Who:

What:

Where:

When:

Why:

Precedent / Genesis:

Most Privileged:

Least Privileged:

WORLDBUILDING THROUGH CULTURE

Are there certain people who can get away with more violence than others?

Who:

What:

Where:

When:

Why:

Precedent / Genesis:

Most Privileged:

Least Privileged:

Is sexual violence abhorred, ignored, or encouraged?

Who:

What:

Where:

When:

Why:

Precedent / Genesis:

Most Privileged:

Least Privileged:

WORLDBUILDING THROUGH CULTURE

Is domestic violence / abuse abhorred, ignored, or encouraged?

Who:

What:

Where:

When:

Why:

Precedent / Genesis:

Most Privileged:

Least Privileged:

Are personal assault and playground violence abhorred, ignored, or encouraged?

Who:

What:

Where:

When:

Why:

Precedent / Genesis:

Most Privileged:

Least Privileged:

WORLDBUILDING THROUGH CULTURE

Does your culture have a concept of war? Has it ever been at war?

Who:

What:

Where:

When:

Why:

Precedent / Genesis:

Most Privileged:

Least Privileged:

Does your culture have a police/law enforcement faction?

Who:

What:

Where:

When:

Why:

Precedent / Genesis:

Most Privileged:

Least Privileged:

WORLDBUILDING THROUGH CULTURE

Does your culture have a concept of murder, or snuffing out a person, or making them "stop"?

Who:

What:

Where:

When:

Why:

Precedent / Genesis:

Most Privileged:

Least Privileged:

How is murder of the self (suicide) regarded, or policed, or prevented?

Who:

What:

Where:

When:

Why:

Precedent / Genesis:

Most Privileged:

Least Privileged:

WORLDBUILDING THROUGH CULTURE

How is the murder of a political figure (assassination or regicide) viewed, prevented, or encouraged?

Who:

What:

Where:

When:

Why:

Precedent / Genesis:

Most Privileged:

Least Privileged:

Is assassination an acceptable way to alter the politics of the world? Does it work?

Who:

What:

Where:

When:

Why:

Precedent / Genesis:

Most Privileged:

Least Privileged:

WORLDBUILDING THROUGH CULTURE

Are protests and riots an acceptable or viable way to affect politics and decisions? Do they work?

Who:

What:

Where:

When:

Why:

Precedent / Genesis:

Most Privileged:

Least Privileged:

CRIME & PUNISHMENT

Are there formal, codified legal rules?

Who:

What:

Where:

When:

Why:

Precedent / Genesis:

Most Privileged:

Least Privileged:

WORLDBUILDING THROUGH CULTURE

Are there levels of seriousness in laws, with escalating punishments based on the severity of the lawbreaking?

Who:

What:

Where:

When:

Why:

Precedent / Genesis:

Most Privileged:

Least Privileged:

Who enforces these rules? How?

Who:

What:

Where:

When:

Why:

Precedent / Genesis:

Most Privileged:

Least Privileged:

WORLDBUILDING THROUGH CULTURE

Is there a mechanism by which rule-enforcers can abuse their power? Do they use it?

Who:

What:

Where:

When:

Why:

Precedent / Genesis:

Most Privileged:

Least Privileged:

Is law enforcement a volunteer position, or a profession?

Who:

What:

Where:

When:

Why:

Precedent / Genesis:

Most Privileged:

Least Privileged:

WORLDBUILDING THROUGH CULTURE

What happens to people who break the rules? Is there corporal punishment? The death sentence? Jails?

Who:

What:

Where:

When:

Why:

Precedent / Genesis:

Most Privileged:

Least Privileged:

Are people punished in public or private?

Who:

What:

Where:

When:

Why:

Precedent / Genesis:

Most Privileged:

Least Privileged:

WORLDBUILDING THROUGH CULTURE

Who has the right to enact the punishment? The person who was wronged? A professional punisher? A witness?

Who:

What:

Where:

When:

Why:

Precedent / Genesis:

Most Privileged:

Least Privileged:

Are those accused of crimes considered immediately guilty, without benefit of trial?

Who:

What:

Where:

When:

Why:

Precedent / Genesis:

Most Privileged:

Least Privileged:

WORLDBUILDING THROUGH CULTURE

Can people plead their cases, or try to prove themselves innocent?

Who:

What:

Where:

When:

Why:

Precedent / Genesis:

Most Privileged:

Least Privileged:

Is someone only guilty if they're caught in the act of breaking a law?

Who:

What:

Where:

When:

Why:

Precedent / Genesis:

Most Privileged:

Least Privileged:

WORLDBUILDING THROUGH CULTURE

Is there any situation in which breaking the law is acceptable?

Who:

What:

Where:

When:

Why:

Precedent / Genesis:

Most Privileged:

Least Privileged:

Who makes the final judgement of guilt / innocence, and the corresponding punishment?

Who:

What:

Where:

When:

Why:

Precedent / Genesis:

Most Privileged:

Least Privileged:

SPIRITUALITY & RELIGION

What is "self"? How is it defined? Is one's "self" separate from one's physical body? Do they believe in souls?

Who:

What:

Where:

When:

Why:

Precedent / Genesis:

Most Privileged:

Least Privileged:

Where does "selfness" reside? (In the head, the heart, or elsewhere in the body?)

Who:

What:

Where:

When:

Why:

Precedent / Genesis:

Most Privileged:

Least Privileged:

WORLDBUILDING THROUGH CULTURE

How do your people explain the natural workings of the world? Has this always been the explanation?

Who:

What:

Where:

When:

Why:

Precedent / Genesis:

Most Privileged:

Least Privileged:

Do they believe in gods, or some sort of higher power? Are they answerable to that power?

Who:

What:

Where:

When:

Why:

Precedent / Genesis:

Most Privileged:

Least Privileged:

WORLDBUILDING THROUGH CULTURE

Are those gods real? Are there people who believe they are, even if they're just constructs of human imagination?

Who:

What:

Where:

When:

Why:

Precedent / Genesis:

Most Privileged:

Least Privileged:

Are there rules meted down from this higher power? How do people punish others who fail to follow them? How does the higher power punish them?

Who:

What:

Where:

When:

Why:

Precedent / Genesis:

Most Privileged:

Least Privileged:

WORLDBUILDING THROUGH CULTURE

Can the higher power be bribed or bargained with? *Must* it be, to get what you want from it?

Who:

What:

Where:

When:

Why:

Precedent / Genesis:

Most Privileged:

Least Privileged:

Is the higher power terrifying, and should their attention be avoided? Is attracting their attention tragic or a danger?

Who:

What:

Where:

When:

Why:

Precedent / Genesis:

Most Privileged:

Least Privileged:

WORLDBUILDING THROUGH CULTURE

What do they believe happens to them when they die? Is there some part of them that lives on in some fashion, or does the meat of their bodies just rot and it's all over?

Who:

What:

Where:

When:

Why:

Precedent / Genesis:

Most Privileged:

Least Privileged:

PROPERTY & POSSESSIONS

How do people think of property and possessions? Do people own things individually? Can they?

Who:

What:

Where:

When:

Why:

Precedent / Genesis:

Most Privileged:

Least Privileged:

WORLDBUILDING THROUGH CULTURE

Who owns what? Does anyone own *anything*?

Who:

What:

Where:

When:

Why:

Precedent / Genesis:

Most Privileged:

Least Privileged:

Is money or barter used to purchase or obtain items, or can people just take / use / ask for what they need?

Who:

What:

Where:

When:

Why:

Precedent / Genesis:

Most Privileged:

Least Privileged:

WORLDBUILDING THROUGH CULTURE

What things are precious, and can be exchanged for other things? Is it metals, or stones, or paper representations of wealth? Is it animals, or land, or trading children, or...?

Who:

What:

Where:

When:

Why:

Precedent / Genesis:

Most Privileged:

Least Privileged:

What happens to thieves, cheats, and liars?

Who:

What:

Where:

When:

Why:

Precedent / Genesis:

Most Privileged:

Least Privileged:

WORLDBUILDING THROUGH CULTURE

How does one reclaim lost or stolen property?

Who:

What:

Where:

When:

Why:

Precedent / Genesis:

Most Privileged:

Least Privileged:

Who is responsible for damages? What if they're the result of a natural disaster or an accident, with no clear person to blame?

Who:

What:

Where:

When:

Why:

Precedent / Genesis:

Most Privileged:

Least Privileged:

WORLDBUILDING THROUGH CULTURE

How is property protected?

Who:

What:

Where:

When:

Why:

Precedent / Genesis:

Most Privileged:

Least Privileged:

Can you buy / own land / water / air / other natural resources?

Who:

What:

Where:

When:

Why:

Precedent / Genesis:

Most Privileged:

Least Privileged:

WORLDBUILDING THROUGH CULTURE

What is shared communally? What's the punishment for taking more than your fair share?

Who:

What:

Where:

When:

Why:

Precedent / Genesis:

Most Privileged:

Least Privileged:

ANIMAL RIGHTS

Are animals considered "people"?

Who:

What:

Where:

When:

Why:

Precedent / Genesis:

Most Privileged:

Least Privileged:

WORLDBUILDING THROUGH CULTURE

Do animals have rights and protections under the law or by tradition? If so, is it all animals, or just some?

Who:

What:

Where:

When:

Why:

Precedent / Genesis:

Most Privileged:

Least Privileged:

Is there a mythological / anecdotal / scientific explanation for the origin of animals, and why they are different from people?

Who:

What:

Where:

When:

Why:

Precedent / Genesis:

Most Privileged:

Least Privileged:

WORLDBUILDING THROUGH CULTURE

Can people own animals?

Who:

What:

Where:

When:

Why:

Precedent / Genesis:

Most Privileged:

Least Privileged:

Are animals used for labour (riding, pulling plow, etc.)

Who:

What:

Where:

When:

Why:

Precedent / Genesis:

Most Privileged:

Least Privileged:

WORLDBUILDING THROUGH CULTURE

Can animals be pets? Are they welcome in the home?

Who:

What:

Where:

When:

Why:

Precedent / Genesis:

Most Privileged:

Least Privileged:

Are people vegetarian or vegan? Do they consume animal products like milk and honey? Do they wait for animals to die naturally or do they hunt / farm / kill animals?

Who:

What:

Where:

When:

Why:

Precedent / Genesis:

Most Privileged:

Least Privileged:

WORLDBUILDING THROUGH CULTURE

Why do they think animals exist? Do they believe animals have souls?

Who:

What:

Where:

When:

Why:

Precedent / Genesis:

Most Privileged:

Least Privileged:

COMMUNITY

Who is considered a part of a "community"? Who is not?

Who:

What:

Where:

When:

Why:

Precedent / Genesis:

Most Privileged:

Least Privileged:

WORLDBUILDING THROUGH CULTURE

How is the social web structured? Who lives with whom?

Who:
___

What:
___

Where:
___

When:
___

Why:
___

Precedent / Genesis:
___

Most Privileged:
___

Least Privileged:
___

What obligations do people have to their community?

Who:

What:

Where:

When:

Why:

Precedent / Genesis:

Most Privileged:

Least Privileged:

WORLDBUILDING THROUGH CULTURE

What obligations does the community have toward an individual?

Who:

What:

Where:

When:

Why:

Precedent / Genesis:

Most Privileged:

Least Privileged:

Do people live together or alone? In what sorts of arrangements and across which gender / sex / age lines?

Who:

What:

Where:

When:

Why:

Precedent / Genesis:

Most Privileged:

Least Privileged:

WORLDBUILDING THROUGH CULTURE

How do people support one another? Do caregiver jobs and positions exist? Does it fall on the family?

Who:

What:

Where:

When:

Why:

Precedent / Genesis:

Most Privileged:

Least Privileged:

What happens to those who are not able to physically or mentally participate in labour / work?

Who:

What:

Where:

When:

Why:

Precedent / Genesis:

Most Privileged:

Least Privileged:

WORLDBUILDING THROUGH CULTURE

At what age are people 'elderly'? What status do they hold in the community? Are they a burden, or revered?

Who:

What:

Where:

When:

Why:

Precedent / Genesis:

Most Privileged:

Least Privileged:

Does everyone share in community work, like harvests and building? Are people employed to work for others?

Who:

What:

Where:

When:

Why:

Precedent / Genesis:

Most Privileged:

Least Privileged:

WORLDBUILDING THROUGH CULTURE

Are there classes or tiers, and who is considered the most enviable in the community? The least?

Who:

What:

Where:

When:

Why:

Precedent / Genesis:

Most Privileged:

Least Privileged:

Can people change classes or tiers? What does it take, and how are people treated when they do?

Who:

What:

Where:

When:

Why:

Precedent / Genesis:

Most Privileged:

Least Privileged:

WORLDBUILDING THROUGH CULTURE

SEX & GENDER

Do they have a concept of "love"? Why? Why not?

Who:

What:

Where:

When:

Why:

Precedent / Genesis:

Most Privileged:

Least Privileged:

Is sex performed while hidden or out in the open? Is it shameful, or celebrated, or neither?

Who:

What:

Where:

When:

Why:

Precedent / Genesis:

Most Privileged:

Least Privileged:

WORLDBUILDING THROUGH CULTURE

Where and when do most people partake in sex? During the day? In public? In private?

Who:

What:

Where:

When:

Why:

Precedent / Genesis:

Most Privileged:

Least Privileged:

Is sex considered an intimate, private act, or is it something shared with friends? Strangers? The public?

Who:

What:

Where:

When:

Why:

Precedent / Genesis:

Most Privileged:

Least Privileged:

WORLDBUILDING THROUGH CULTURE

What are the rules about who can have sex with whom?

Who:

What:

Where:

When:

Why:

Precedent / Genesis:

Most Privileged:

Least Privileged:

Is biological sex equated with gender? Is it a binary or a sliding scale?

Who:

What:

Where:

When:

Why:

Precedent / Genesis:

Most Privileged:

Least Privileged:

WORLDBUILDING THROUGH CULTURE

How many genders and biological sexes does your culture acknowledge?

Who:

What:

Where:

When:

Why:

Precedent / Genesis:

Most Privileged:

Least Privileged:

What is the traditional explanation for this? Spiritual? Medical? Is there a taboo surrounding some of these?

Who:

What:

Where:

When:

Why:

Precedent / Genesis:

Most Privileged:

Least Privileged:

WORLDBUILDING THROUGH CULTURE

Is sex engaged in only for pleasure? Procreation? Both?

Who:

What:

Where:

When:

Why:

Precedent / Genesis:

Most Privileged:

Least Privileged:

How are sexual partners/groups chosen? Who gets the ability to choose? Who doesn't?

Who:

What:

Where:

When:

Why:

Precedent / Genesis:

Most Privileged:

Least Privileged:

WORLDBUILDING THROUGH CULTURE

What are the issues, laws, and traditions around sexual consent?

Who:

What:

Where:

When:

Why:

Precedent / Genesis:

Most Privileged:

Least Privileged:

At what age / stage of life are people considered wise and responsible enough to engage in sex?

Who:

What:

Where:

When:

Why:

Precedent / Genesis:

Most Privileged:

Least Privileged:

WORLDBUILDING THROUGH CULTURE

What does society think of people who choose not to engage in sex?

Who:

What:

Where:

When:

Why:

Precedent / Genesis:

Most Privileged:

Least Privileged:

Do sex crimes exist, and what constitutes one? What is the punishment for raping a woman? A man? A child?

Who:

What:

Where:

When:

Why:

Precedent / Genesis:

Most Privileged:

Least Privileged:

WORLDBUILDING THROUGH CULTURE

What are the discussions surrounding consent and assault? What constitutes consent or assault?

Who:

What:

Where:

When:

Why:

Precedent / Genesis:

Most Privileged:

Least Privileged:

Do they let love dictate their relationships, choices or hierarchies?

Who:

What:

Where:

When:

Why:

Precedent / Genesis:

Most Privileged:

Least Privileged:

WORLDBUILDING THROUGH CULTURE

Who is allowed to love whom? Are there rules based on class, gender, sex, race, ethnicity, religion, etc.?

Who:

What:

Where:

When:

Why:

Precedent / Genesis:

Most Privileged:

Least Privileged:

Is one gender or biological sex considered more promiscuous or sexually aggressive than another?

Who:

What:

Where:

When:

Why:

Precedent / Genesis:

Most Privileged:

Least Privileged:

FRIENDSHIP

How are strong friendships different from romantic relationships? What's the difference?

Who:

What:

Where:

When:

Why:

Precedent / Genesis:

Most Privileged:

Least Privileged:

Are there rules about who gets to be friends with whom, based on age, gender, sex, race, class, etc.?

Who:

What:

Where:

When:

Why:

Precedent / Genesis:

Most Privileged:

Least Privileged:

WORLDBUILDING THROUGH CULTURE

How do people greet a friend? How do they greet a lover? Is it different? Why?

Who:

What:

Where:

When:

Why:

Precedent / Genesis:

Most Privileged:

Least Privileged:

How physical can friends be with one another? Hold hands? Kiss on the cheek? Share a bed? Walk closely?

Who:

What:

Where:

When:

Why:

Precedent / Genesis:

Most Privileged:

Least Privileged:

Is there any sort of formal ceremony marking the start or end of a friendship?

Who:

What:

Where:

When:

Why:

Precedent / Genesis:

Most Privileged:

Least Privileged:

How "deep" is a friendship? How shallow?

Who:

What:

Where:

When:

Why:

Precedent / Genesis:

Most Privileged:

Least Privileged:

WORLDBUILDING THROUGH CULTURE

What are friends expected to do when another marries? Has children? Dies? Are there traditions and rites?

Who:

What:

Where:

When:

Why:

Precedent / Genesis:

Most Privileged:

Least Privileged:

ROMANCE

How is courtship structured? What are the rituals?

Who:

What:

Where:

When:

Why:

Precedent / Genesis:

Most Privileged:

Least Privileged:

WORLDBUILDING THROUGH CULTURE

Can people engage in sex before marriage?

Who:

What:

Where:

When:

Why:

Precedent / Genesis:

Most Privileged:

Least Privileged:

Who chooses the participants in a marriage? Their parents? Their friends? Themselves? Why?

Who:

What:

Where:

When:

Why:

Precedent / Genesis:

Most Privileged:

Least Privileged:

WORLDBUILDING THROUGH CULTURE

Are marriages arranged? By whom, and when, and why? If not, why not?

Who:

What:

Where:

When:

Why:

Precedent / Genesis:

Most Privileged:

Least Privileged:

Are participants in a marriage active or passive in choosing their spouse?

Who:

What:

Where:

When:

Why:

Precedent / Genesis:

Most Privileged:

Least Privileged:

WORLDBUILDING THROUGH CULTURE

Who chases and who is chased? Who selects, and who is selected?

Who:

What:

Where:

When:

Why:

Precedent / Genesis:

Most Privileged:

Least Privileged:

How many people are involved in a marriage, and what is the legal definition of a marriage?

Who:

What:

Where:

When:

Why:

Precedent / Genesis:

Most Privileged:

Least Privileged:

WORLDBUILDING THROUGH CULTURE

Are marriages between certain kinds of people not allowed? What happens if they shack up anyway?

Who:

What:

Where:

When:

Why:

Precedent / Genesis:

Most Privileged:

Least Privileged:

Can widow(ers) remarry?

Who:

What:

Where:

When:

Why:

Precedent / Genesis:

Most Privileged:

Least Privileged:

WORLDBUILDING THROUGH CULTURE

Can a marriage end in a divorce? Or only in death? *Does* it end in death, or is the marriage still active if one person is dead?

Who:

What:

Where:

When:

Why:

Precedent / Genesis:

Most Privileged:

Least Privileged:

What celebrations and shames surround marriage oaths and/or the breaking of them?

Who:

What:

Where:

When:

Why:

Precedent / Genesis:

Most Privileged:

Least Privileged:

WORLDBUILDING THROUGH CULTURE

Is monogamy expected or valued in a marriage? Why or why not?

Who:

What:

Where:

When:

Why:

Precedent / Genesis:

Most Privileged:

Least Privileged:

CHILDREARING

How do they believe children are conceived? How are children *actually* conceived? (Sex? Magic? Science?)

Who:

What:

Where:

When:

Why:

Precedent / Genesis:

Most Privileged:

Least Privileged:

WORLDBUILDING THROUGH CULTURE

What is the medical explanation for how pregnancies happen? The mystical? Are they the same?

Who:

What:

Where:

When:

Why:

Precedent / Genesis:

Most Privileged:

Least Privileged:

How do pregnancies and gestation periods go? What's the timeline, who carries, what does birth look like?

Who:

What:

Where:

When:

Why:

Precedent / Genesis:

Most Privileged:

Least Privileged:

WORLDBUILDING THROUGH CULTURE

What is the tradition around birthing children? Who is present, and who, if anyone, is excluded?

Who:

What:

Where:

When:

Why:

Precedent / Genesis:

Most Privileged:

Least Privileged:

How are children reared? Who has primary responsibility?

Who:

What:

Where:

When:

Why:

Precedent / Genesis:

Most Privileged:

Least Privileged:

WORLDBUILDING THROUGH CULTURE

To whom do children belong? Whose responsibility is it to raise them and educate them?

Who:

What:

Where:

When:

Why:

Precedent / Genesis:

Most Privileged:

Least Privileged:

Are children "owned" or considered their own person?

Who:

What:

Where:

When:

Why:

Precedent / Genesis:

Most Privileged:

Least Privileged:

WORLDBUILDING THROUGH CULTURE

At what age are children considered adults?

Who:

What:

Where:

When:

Why:

Precedent / Genesis:

Most Privileged:

Least Privileged:

Do children have to perform a task or reach a milestone to be independent, and in charge of their own agency?

Who:

What:

Where:

When:

Why:

Precedent / Genesis:

Most Privileged:

Least Privileged:

WORLDBUILDING THROUGH CULTURE

Does your society have a concept of "bastards"? Are they shunned, or killed, or loved all the same?

Who:

What:

Where:

When:

Why:

Precedent / Genesis:

Most Privileged:

Least Privileged:

How are children with disabilities cared for?

Who:

What:

Where:

When:

Why:

Precedent / Genesis:

Most Privileged:

Least Privileged:

WORLDBUILDING THROUGH CULTURE

How are unwanted pregnancies defined and terminated? Who has access to terminations? Legally? In actuality?

Who:

What:

Where:

When:

Why:

Precedent / Genesis:

Most Privileged:

Least Privileged:

At what point in the gestation period are fetuses considered "persons" under the law, and does their bodily autonomy supersede that of the carrying parent?

Who:

What:

Where:

When:

Why:

Precedent / Genesis:

Most Privileged:

Least Privileged:

WORLDBUILDING THROUGH CULTURE

EDUCATION

Is there a community-wide system of formal learning?

Who:

What:

Where:

When:

Why:

Precedent / Genesis:

Most Privileged:

Least Privileged:

Who receives a general education? What lessons are considered core skills?

Who:

What:

Where:

When:

Why:

Precedent / Genesis:

Most Privileged:

Least Privileged:

WORLDBUILDING THROUGH CULTURE

At what age or milestone do people begin to be educated? How long does schooling last?

Who:

What:

Where:

When:

Why:

Precedent / Genesis:

Most Privileged:

Least Privileged:

Is there learning that is considered taboo, or only for the elite, or certain classes, etc.?

Who:

What:

Where:

When:

Why:

Precedent / Genesis:

Most Privileged:

Least Privileged:

WORLDBUILDING THROUGH CULTURE

Who is responsible for teaching, and how and where are they trained to teach? (If they're trained at all.)

Who:

What:

Where:

When:

Why:

Precedent / Genesis:

Most Privileged:

Least Privileged:

J.M. FREY

What information is considered vital for people to know outside of a general education?

Who:

What:

Where:

When:

Why:

Precedent / Genesis:

Most Privileged:

Least Privileged:

WORLDBUILDING THROUGH CULTURE

How is this vital information shared?

Who:

What:

Where:

When:

Why:

Precedent / Genesis:

Most Privileged:

Least Privileged:

Does your station / gender / race / sex / creed affect what you're taught or allowed to know?

Who:

What:

Where:

When:

Why:

Precedent / Genesis:

Most Privileged:

Least Privileged:

WORLDBUILDING THROUGH CULTURE

Are there rules about who learns what, and from whom? Or where?

Who:

What:

Where:

When:

Why:

Precedent / Genesis:

Most Privileged:

Least Privileged:

LEISURE

What do your people do for fun?

Who:

What:

Where:

When:

Why:

Precedent / Genesis:

Most Privileged:

Least Privileged:

WORLDBUILDING THROUGH CULTURE

Do your people consume intoxicants or hallucinogens?

Who:

What:

Where:

When:

Why:

Precedent / Genesis:

Most Privileged:

Least Privileged:

Do your people feast? Why or why not?

Who:

What:

Where:

When:

Why:

Precedent / Genesis:

Most Privileged:

Least Privileged:

WORLDBUILDING THROUGH CULTURE

What do they eat on special days?

Who:

What:

Where:

When:

Why:

Precedent / Genesis:

Most Privileged:

Least Privileged:

How are stories shared? Through song and dance? Storytelling? Through words, fiction, poetry, scrolls, reading tablets or computers?

Who:

What:

Where:

When:

Why:

Precedent / Genesis:

Most Privileged:

Least Privileged:

WORLDBUILDING THROUGH CULTURE

Do they enjoy music, or theatre? Do they watch others perform or play-act, or demonstrate their talents? Or is creation private?

Who:

What:

Where:

When:

Why:

Precedent / Genesis:

Most Privileged:

Least Privileged:

Is there a celebrity culture?

Who:

What:

Where:

When:

Why:

Precedent / Genesis:

Most Privileged:

Least Privileged:

WORLDBUILDING THROUGH CULTURE

Do they hold sporting events? Are there formalized, organized sports?

Who:

What:

Where:

When:

Why:

Precedent / Genesis:

Most Privileged:

Least Privileged:

Who participates in sporting events? Are there observers? Audiences? Are there teams to cheer for?

Who:

What:

Where:

When:

Why:

Precedent / Genesis:

Most Privileged:

Least Privileged:

WORLDBUILDING THROUGH CULTURE

Is the entertainment government sanctioned? Is it required that all attend? What happens if they don't?

Who:

What:

Where:

When:

Why:

Precedent / Genesis:

Most Privileged:

Least Privileged:

Is there Paid Time Off and set days of the week for rest?

Who:

What:

Where:

When:

Why:

Precedent / Genesis:

Most Privileged:

Least Privileged:

WORLDBUILDING THROUGH CULTURE

Is what children do for fun the same as what adults do?

Who:

What:

Where:

When:

Why:

Precedent / Genesis:

Most Privileged:

Least Privileged:

Does your society celebrate play, or find it childish and something to grow out of?

Who:

What:

Where:

When:

Why:

Precedent / Genesis:

Most Privileged:

Least Privileged:

WORLDBUILDING THROUGH CULTURE

THE ARTS

How do people try to celebrate and explain their "selfness" through the arts?

Who:

What:

Where:

When:

Why:

Precedent / Genesis:

Most Privileged:

Least Privileged:

How do people try to celebrate and explain the natural world through the arts?

Who:

What:

Where:

When:

Why:

Precedent / Genesis:

Most Privileged:

Least Privileged:

WORLDBUILDING THROUGH CULTURE

Is music a thing? Do people sing? Is this accepted? Allowed? Forbidden? Encouraged?

Who:

What:

Where:

When:

Why:

Precedent / Genesis:

Most Privileged:

Least Privileged:

What kind of instruments do they make / use?

Who:

What:

Where:

When:

Why:

Precedent / Genesis:

Most Privileged:

Least Privileged:

WORLDBUILDING THROUGH CULTURE

How do they write the language of music in order to share songs?

Who:

What:

Where:

When:

Why:

Precedent / Genesis:

Most Privileged:

Least Privileged:

Do people paint / draw?

Who:

What:

Where:

When:

Why:

Precedent / Genesis:

Most Privileged:

Least Privileged:

WORLDBUILDING THROUGH CULTURE

What materials do they use to create visual art?

Who:

What:

Where:

When:

Why:

Precedent / Genesis:

Most Privileged:

Least Privileged:

Do they write down stories? How and why? How are they disseminated if they do? Is there a form of publishing?

Who:

What:

Where:

When:

Why:

Precedent / Genesis:

Most Privileged:

Least Privileged:

WORLDBUILDING THROUGH CULTURE

What is the etiquette for audience members attending a live performance?

Who:

What:

Where:

When:

Why:

Precedent / Genesis:

Most Privileged:

Least Privileged:

How do audience members show appreciation or disdain for a performance? Is it different if it's live or recorded?

Who:

What:

Where:

When:

Why:

Precedent / Genesis:

Most Privileged:

Least Privileged:

WORLDBUILDING THROUGH CULTURE

How and when do people enjoy performances such as Theatre or Opera? Live? Only through a screen?

Who:

What:

Where:

When:

Why:

Precedent / Genesis:

Most Privileged:

Least Privileged:

When are the arts usually enjoyed? Privately or publicly?

Who:

What:

Where:

When:

Why:

Precedent / Genesis:

Most Privileged:

Least Privileged:

WORLDBUILDING THROUGH CULTURE

Are there any topics that are considered forbidden, or taboo, or too unseemly for the arts?

Who:

What:

Where:

When:

Why:

Precedent / Genesis:

Most Privileged:

Least Privileged:

Can one own artistic works, books, song sheets, paintings, instruments, etc.?

Who:

What:

Where:

When:

Why:

Precedent / Genesis:

Most Privileged:

Least Privileged:

WORLDBUILDING THROUGH CULTURE

Who sanctions art? Is it controlled by the government or taste-masters? Or can creators make whatever they want?

Who:

What:

Where:

When:

Why:

Precedent / Genesis:

Most Privileged:

Least Privileged:

Are the arts being used for government propaganda? Overtly, or unknowingly to the populace?

Who:

What:

Where:

When:

Why:

Precedent / Genesis:

Most Privileged:

Least Privileged:

WORLDBUILDING THROUGH CULTURE

Do amateurs make music / art / stories / plays for fun?

Who:

What:

Where:

When:

Why:

Precedent / Genesis:

Most Privileged:

Least Privileged:

How do professional artists get paid or compensated? Patrons? Government Sponsorship? Commissions?

Who:

What:

Where:

When:

Why:

Precedent / Genesis:

Most Privileged:

Least Privileged:

WORLDBUILDING THROUGH CULTURE

Do people have to pay to access the arts? Everything? Just some things? Does that affect the quality of the thing?

Who:

What:

Where:

When:

Why:

Precedent / Genesis:

Most Privileged:

Least Privileged:

Is there a concept of "copyright"? Do artists own what they create? Can they at all? Must they register it?

Who:

What:

Where:

When:

Why:

Precedent / Genesis:

Most Privileged:

Least Privileged:

WORLDBUILDING THROUGH CULTURE

How are art pieces shared outside of context / a gallery / a theatre / a poetry reading / etc.? Can people access art on the go, or in their homes?

Who:

What:

Where:

When:

Why:

Precedent / Genesis:

Most Privileged:

Least Privileged:

Is being a professional artist considered a job? Does one train / apprentice for it?

Who:

What:

Where:

When:

Why:

Precedent / Genesis:

Most Privileged:

Least Privileged:

SPORT & ACTIVITY

Do people play organized games? Who organizes them? Who sets the rules?

Who:

What:

Where:

When:

Why:

Precedent / Genesis:

Most Privileged:

Least Privileged:

Are most sports designed to showcase individual merit (like speed skating), to showcase artistic talent (like figure skating), to showcase group cohesion and planning (like hockey), or to encourage bonding and comradery (like shinny).

Who:

What:

Where:

When:

Why:

Precedent / Genesis:

Most Privileged:

Least Privileged:

WORLDBUILDING THROUGH CULTURE

Are games only professional? Are they amateur and between families, clans, neighbourhoods, etc.? Both?

Who:

What:

Where:

When:

Why:

Precedent / Genesis:

Most Privileged:

Least Privileged:

How are teams decided, and how can you tell them apart?

Who:
___

What:
___

Where:
___

When:
___

Why:
___

Precedent / Genesis:
___

Most Privileged:
___

Least Privileged:
___

WORLDBUILDING THROUGH CULTURE

Do people support specific teams? Does it carry into their real lives? Do they wear team colours to show support?

Who:

What:

Where:

When:

Why:

Precedent / Genesis:

Most Privileged:

Least Privileged:

Do games stand in for war? Do the outcomes of the games actually affect society and policy?

Who:

What:

Where:

When:

Why:

Precedent / Genesis:

Most Privileged:

Least Privileged:

Do people exercise for health, or vanity reasons? Or at all?

Who:

What:

Where:

When:

Why:

Precedent / Genesis:

Most Privileged:

Least Privileged:

Are athletes paid? Do they choose and fight to compete, or are they forced to?

Who:

What:

Where:

When:

Why:

Precedent / Genesis:

Most Privileged:

Least Privileged:

WORLDBUILDING THROUGH CULTURE

Are there children's games that are meant to teach them lessons, rules, or laws?

Who:

What:

Where:

When:

Why:

Precedent / Genesis:

Most Privileged:

Least Privileged:

SYSTEMS OF PAYMENT

Are there concepts of "wealth" and "poverty"?

Who:

What:

Where:

When:

Why:

Precedent / Genesis:

Most Privileged:

Least Privileged:

WORLDBUILDING THROUGH CULTURE

Who lives in poverty? Who in wealth?

Who:

What:

Where:

When:

Why:

Precedent / Genesis:

Most Privileged:

Least Privileged:

Are the wealthy considered greedy or enviable?

Who:

What:

Where:

When:

Why:

Precedent / Genesis:

Most Privileged:

Least Privileged:

WORLDBUILDING THROUGH CULTURE

How are necessities shared? Buy it? Get it free? Everyone chips in and shares?

Who:

What:

Where:

When:

Why:

Precedent / Genesis:

Most Privileged:

Least Privileged:

Are people paid for their labour? Paid in what, and at what rate?

Who:

What:

Where:

When:

Why:

Precedent / Genesis:

Most Privileged:

Least Privileged:

WORLDBUILDING THROUGH CULTURE

Do they have a concept of "money" or representational wealth?

Who:

What:

Where:

When:

Why:

Precedent / Genesis:

Most Privileged:

Least Privileged:

How do people "pay" for things? Do they barter? Or exchange promises or labour, precious metals, or abstract representations like paper money or digital credits?

Who:

What:

Where:

When:

Why:

Precedent / Genesis:

Most Privileged:

Least Privileged:

WORLDBUILDING THROUGH CULTURE

Can people be used for payment? Animals?

Who:

What:

Where:

When:

Why:

Precedent / Genesis:

Most Privileged:

Least Privileged:

How does one pay for food? Clothing? Rent? Utilities? Is it all the same, or different systems / money?

Who:

What:

Where:

When:

Why:

Precedent / Genesis:

Most Privileged:

Least Privileged:

WORLDBUILDING THROUGH CULTURE

What is considered the rarest and most valuable item, that people would give anything to own or would be considered wealthy if they had it?

Who:

What:

Where:

When:

Why:

Precedent / Genesis:

Most Privileged:

Least Privileged:

How is theft or cheating on payments punished?

Who:

What:

Where:

When:

Why:

Precedent / Genesis:

Most Privileged:

Least Privileged:

WORLDBUILDING THROUGH CULTURE

How are shopkeepers punished for cheating customers?

Who:

What:

Where:

When:

Why:

Precedent / Genesis:

Most Privileged:

Least Privileged:

How are prices indicated, and written out in shops?

Who:

What:

Where:

When:

Why:

Precedent / Genesis:

Most Privileged:

Least Privileged:

NOBILITY & ROYALTY

Is there a concept of people from certain families or bloodlines being better / higher / closer to god / naturally born leaders / having the right to rule?

Who:

What:

Where:

When:

Why:

Precedent / Genesis:

Most Privileged:

Least Privileged:

Who and what decides that these people are special?

Who:

What:

Where:

When:

Why:

Precedent / Genesis:

Most Privileged:

Least Privileged:

WORLDBUILDING THROUGH CULTURE

What happens when other people disagree about who is special, and who is not?

Who:

What:

Where:

When:

Why:

Precedent / Genesis:

Most Privileged:

Least Privileged:

What rules must be followed to be considered noble or royal? What eligibilities or requirements are there?

Who:

What:

Where:

When:

Why:

Precedent / Genesis:

Most Privileged:

Least Privileged:

WORLDBUILDING THROUGH CULTURE

How far out on the family tree limbs do you have to get before you go from "royal" to "commoner"?

Who:

What:

Where:

When:

Why:

Precedent / Genesis:

Most Privileged:

Least Privileged:

What special privileges and / or perks does the royalty or nobility enjoy?

Who:

What:

Where:

When:

Why:

Precedent / Genesis:

Most Privileged:

Least Privileged:

WORLDBUILDING THROUGH CULTURE

What special trials and sacrifices must the royalty or nobility endure?

Who:

What:

Where:

When:

Why:

Precedent / Genesis:

Most Privileged:

Least Privileged:

What things are your nobility and royalty not allowed to do, which everyone else is?

Who:

What:

Where:

When:

Why:

Precedent / Genesis:

Most Privileged:

Least Privileged:

WORLDBUILDING THROUGH CULTURE

Does the nobility / royalty live separately from commoners? Do they live in the same dwellings, or same part of town?

Who:

What:

Where:

When:

Why:

Precedent / Genesis:

Most Privileged:

Least Privileged:

Can nobility / royalty be deposed? Under what circumstances, and how is it done?

Who:

What:

Where:

When:

Why:

Precedent / Genesis:

Most Privileged:

Least Privileged:

WORLDBUILDING THROUGH CULTURE

Do they have any involvement in actual governance and lawmaking, or warmongering? Is it all symbolic? Or is it Constitutional? Some form of hybrid governance?

Who:

What:

Where:

When:

Why:

Precedent / Genesis:

Most Privileged:

Least Privileged:

Can new noble / royal titles be created? How and by whom?

Who:

What:

Where:

When:

Why:

Precedent / Genesis:

Most Privileged:

Least Privileged:

WORLDBUILDING THROUGH CULTURE

Can people be demoted or promoted in noble rank? How and why?

Who:

What:

Where:

When:

Why:

Precedent / Genesis:

Most Privileged:

Least Privileged:

What extra things do the nobility owe the monarch in exchange for their titles and special treatment?

Who:

What:

Where:

When:

Why:

Precedent / Genesis:

Most Privileged:

Least Privileged:

WORLDBUILDING THROUGH CULTURE

What things do the nobility / royalty owe the common people to retain their titles and special treatment?

Who:

What:

Where:

When:

Why:

Precedent / Genesis:

Most Privileged:

Least Privileged:

TRAVEL

Why would someone need to leave home? Marriage? Political gain? Searching for supplies / food / work?

Who:

What:

Where:

When:

Why:

Precedent / Genesis:

Most Privileged:

Least Privileged:

WORLDBUILDING THROUGH CULTURE

Do people ever need to leave their home to trade for work, or to have meetings elsewhere, or to hold conferences?

Who:

What:

Where:

When:

Why:

Precedent / Genesis:

Most Privileged:

Least Privileged:

What are the normal modes of transportation and how long do they take?

Who:

What:

Where:

When:

Why:

Precedent / Genesis:

Most Privileged:

Least Privileged:

WORLDBUILDING THROUGH CULTURE

Do your people have cartography? Can everyone read maps? Who is allowed to own or buy maps?

Who:

What:

Where:

When:

Why:

Precedent / Genesis:

Most Privileged:

Least Privileged:

Is your whole world mapped by the people who live in it? Or only part of it?

Who:

What:

Where:

When:

Why:

Precedent / Genesis:

Most Privileged:

Least Privileged:

WORLDBUILDING THROUGH CULTURE

Does your culture try to spread? Is it an Empire? Do they colonize, or conquer, or settle?

Who:

What:

Where:

When:

Why:

Precedent / Genesis:

Most Privileged:

Least Privileged:

Are they themselves occupied? Was it peaceful, or insidious, or traumatizing? How was it achieved?

Who:

What:

Where:

When:

Why:

Precedent / Genesis:

Most Privileged:

Least Privileged:

WORLDBUILDING THROUGH CULTURE

Do they have concepts of colonialism and racism? Are they the perpetrators or victims of either?

Who:

What:

Where:

When:

Why:

Precedent / Genesis:

Most Privileged:

Least Privileged:

Is there a concept of travelling for pleasure and / or sightseeing?

Who:

What:

Where:

When:

Why:

Precedent / Genesis:

Most Privileged:

Least Privileged:

WORLDBUILDING THROUGH CULTURE

What sort of places do they go? What attracts visitors? Landscapes, art, locations of historical significance, etc.?

Who:

What:

Where:

When:

Why:

Precedent / Genesis:

Most Privileged:

Least Privileged:

D people only go somewhere there because someone set up a resort / camp / tourist attraction?

Who:

What:

Where:

When:

Why:

Precedent / Genesis:

Most Privileged:

Least Privileged:

WORLDBUILDING THROUGH CULTURE

Is tourism a threat to the environment / native species / population in any of the attractive locales?

Who:

What:

Where:

When:

Why:

Precedent / Genesis:

Most Privileged:

Least Privileged:

What souvenirs do people get? What do they buy, or what are they gifted? What do they steal?

Who:

What:

Where:

When:

Why:

Precedent / Genesis:

Most Privileged:

Least Privileged:

WORLDBUILDING THROUGH CULTURE

Do people ever return home to live? Why or why not? Are they celebrated or shamed for returning?

Who:

What:

Where:

When:

Why:

Precedent / Genesis:

Most Privileged:

Least Privileged:

FADS, TRENDS & DISSEMINATION OF INFLUENCE

Do people follow fashions and fads?

Who:

What:

Where:

When:

Why:

Precedent / Genesis:

Most Privileged:

Least Privileged:

WORLDBUILDING THROUGH CULTURE

How long do fads generally last?

Who:

What:

Where:

When:

Why:

Precedent / Genesis:

Most Privileged:

Least Privileged:

Do they apply to all the arts (fashion, cuisine, decor, etc.)?

Who:

What:

Where:

When:

Why:

Precedent / Genesis:

Most Privileged:

Least Privileged:

WORLDBUILDING THROUGH CULTURE

How do people receive information about new fashions and fads?

Who:

What:

Where:

When:

Why:

Precedent / Genesis:

Most Privileged:

Least Privileged:

Is there a difference in taste between generations, sexes, genders, religions, or ethnicities?

Who:

What:

Where:

When:

Why:

Precedent / Genesis:

Most Privileged:

Least Privileged:

WORLDBUILDING THROUGH CULTURE

Who are the influencers?

Who:

What:

Where:

When:

Why:

Precedent / Genesis:

Most Privileged:

Least Privileged:

How or why are influencers copied? Is there punishment for copying? Or praise?

Who:

What:

Where:

When:

Why:

Precedent / Genesis:

Most Privileged:

Least Privileged:

WORLDBUILDING THROUGH CULTURE

Do people spend money to copy / follow the advice of an influencer?

Who:

What:

Where:

When:

Why:

Precedent / Genesis:

Most Privileged:

Least Privileged:

Is there a concept of 'knock-offs' or cheaper imitations? Are they legal? Encouraged? Considered rude?

Who:

What:

Where:

When:

Why:

Precedent / Genesis:

Most Privileged:

Least Privileged:

WORLDBUILDING THROUGH CULTURE

CELEBRITY & GOSSIP MONGERING

Are there specific people that the general population are all aware of? Do they follow their lives and actions?

Who:

What:

Where:

When:

Why:

Precedent / Genesis:

Most Privileged:

Least Privileged:

How does the general populace get information about celebrities? Magazines? Whispered tales from servants?

Who:

What:

Where:

When:

Why:

Precedent / Genesis:

Most Privileged:

Least Privileged:

WORLDBUILDING THROUGH CULTURE

Who are superstar celebrities? Artists or Athletes? Politicians or nobility? The very clever? The very stupid?

Who:

What:

Where:

When:

Why:

Precedent / Genesis:

Most Privileged:

Least Privileged:

How are people rewarded for achieving celebrity status? Money? A title? Just intangibles like fame?

Who:

What:

Where:

When:

Why:

Precedent / Genesis:

Most Privileged:

Least Privileged:

WORLDBUILDING THROUGH CULTURE

Is becoming a celebrity or famous enviable and desired?

Who:

What:

Where:

When:

Why:

Precedent / Genesis:

Most Privileged:

Least Privileged:

What are the downsides or dangers of becoming a celebrity?

Who:

What:

Where:

When:

Why:

Precedent / Genesis:

Most Privileged:

Least Privileged:

THE SLIDING SCALE

Now that you've got a more thorough understanding of the morals and minutiae of your culture, it's time to add one last dimension to your understanding: the *weight* of them.

By thinking about how the laws, morals, and taboos of your culture are applied to people in different socioeconomic situations in the culture, you've already been thinking about it on a sliding scale of application. Now, I want you to take a step back and look at the whole of your society as if it was, indeed, a monolith–that is, if you looked at the most average, normal, integrated person of the society, and determined their average behaviour, where would they fall on a scale?

Based on the theory of Cultural Dimensions developed by Geert Hofstede[19], I've put together a collection of binary concepts for you to review. Keep in mind that absolutely average citizen of your culture, and make a mark where you think their experience and expectations land on the scale.

Be aware that while these scales represent binary opposites, one extreme is not *better* than the other. These are not value judgements, simply contrasting concepts.

---

[19] Hofstede, Geert. *Cultures and Organizations: Software of the Mind.* (McGraw Hill; 3rd edition 2010).

Mark where your fictional culture generally lands on the sliding scale:

Individual   **Group**

◀ — — — — — — — — — — — — — — ▶

Whose happiness is top of mind when making decisions? Do people do what's best for the harmony and safety of the group, or what's best for their own personal dreams?

Egalitarian   **Hierarchical**

◀ — — — — — — — — — — — — — — ▶

Is anyone more important than others? Is there a strict, codified system of special-ness, or is everyone's individual worth, values, and desires equally valued?

Direct   **Indirect**

◀ — — — — — — — — — — — — — — ▶

When communicating, how blunt are people? Is it polite to say what you really mean/want, or is it rude? Are there euphemisms to discuss unpleasant topics, or roundabout ways of saying no?

Relationship   **Merit**

◀ — — — — — — — — — — — — — — ▶

How is success achieved? Are promotions, advantageous marriages, and favours granted because of who people are and who they know, or because of their work ethic and skillset?

Romance   **Contract**

◀─────────────────▶

How are legal partnerships viewed? Why do marriages exist, and do they offer legal benefits? Are partnerships established by the individuals involved, or by the state?

Irredeemable   **Rehabilitable**

◀─────────────────▶

Do they believe that wrongdoers are redeemable? Are they born evil? Or is it believed people are pressed into or learn to be evil, and therefore can become good again?

Private   **Public**

◀─────────────────▶

Are people allowed to express opinions in public? How far is too far in terms of affection? Are the meetings of government and court rulings available to read? In how much detail? How much of daily life is lived or enjoyed out of doors?

Perfect Democracy   **Absolute Monarchy**

◀─────────────────▶

Who holds the power? How democratic is the governing system? Does everyone get a vote, and is it rigged? How much personal power does the head of state wield, and is it tempered in any way by law or government? How is power distributed and transitioned?

Fast   **Slow**

◄ — — — — — — — — — — — — — — — ►

What is the pace of living? The speed of communication? How urgent are everyday things? Is slowing down a luxury, or an expectation? Is dining an inconvenience or indulgent pageantry? Do people marry young?

Progress   **Stagnation**

◄ — — — — — — — — — — — — — — — ►

How keen are people to adopt the newest trends and technologies? Is there pushback about too much, too fast? Is there frustration about those holding society back?

Extravagant   **Frugal**

◄ — — — — — — — — — — — — — — — ►

Is it considered morally superior to hoard wealth or to spend it? Do people spend excess wealth on personal frivolities, or in enriching their community? Do people spend showily or subtly? Do people save for the future?

Agrarian   **Urban**

◄ — — — — — — — — — — — — — — — ►

Is there a moral superiority associated with where one lives? An aesthetic one? Is most of the population centred in one area over another? Is there an idealized, unrealistic preference for one over another?

Aesthetic   **Spartan**

◄ — — — — — — — — — — — — — — ►

How important are art and decoration? How important is being educated and opinionated about art? Is fussiness valued in food, fashion, and decor, or is minimalism?

Structured   **Free-flowing**

◄ — — — — — — — — — — — — — — ►

How rigidly are places, events, lives, and art planned? Do they go with the flow? Do people celebrate randomness? Are life milestones rigidly enforced?

Religious   **Agnostic**

◄ — — — — — — — — — — — — — — ►

Are faith, belief, ritual, and worship a daily part of the lives of your people? Is it only weekly? Monthly? Seasonal? Do the unknowable things in life enchant them or are they ignored? Do they do anything to acknowledge the possibility of unseen forces or creatures?

Long Term   **Short Term**

◄ — — — — — — — — — — — — — — ►

Do your people plan for the future? Or are they all about gratification in the present? Is stockpiling seen as wise or selfish? Do they have retirement or contingency plans? Do they take joy in the ephemerality of existence and celebrate the present?

LANGUAGE AND DIALOGUE

Just because you're writing a secondary-world tale, it doesn't mean you need to invent a whole new language. You can if you really want to, but as those who do it full time for television and film will tell you, figuring out the rules and structure of something like Klingon or High Valyrian is complicated, takes a great deal of study on the structure of languages, and inventiveness.

Luckily as a writer, there are other, less time-consuming ways of indicating or subtly conveying a foreign culture through word choice, and sentence structure.

You can sprinkle in foreign words that you make up, or slightly altered versions of a familiar word, the way that "kriff" is substituted for profanity in the *Star Wars* universe[20]. Or you can play with word order, making it clear that the speaker is using the grammar rules of their native

---

[20] "List of Phrases and Slang". *Wookiepedia.org*, <https://starwars.fandom.com/wiki/List_of_phrases_and_slang> Accessed: 09/12/2022.

language, like Yoda's famous: "The greatest teacher, failure is."[21]

You can also indicate unfamiliarity with a language through intentionally written dialogue mistakes drawn from:

- Malapropisms
    - Use of an incorrect word in the place of a similar-sounding word.
    - "She's the pineapple of class." (Should be 'pinnacle')
- Jumbled Metaphors and Idioms
    - Incorrect or mixed up common sayings.
    - "Never burn your bridges before they hatch."
- Synonyms
    - Two different words that mean almost the exact same thing, but one is more awkward or less well-known than another.
    - "Look at that murder."
    "That what?!"
    "That flock of crows over there."
- Contranyms
    - Using a word that has two opposing meanings.
    - Depending on how it's used, "Sanction" can mean both 'to approve or allow', and also 'to penalize'.

---

[21] Johnsan, Rian (dir). *Star Wars Episode VIII: The Last Jedi.* (Lucasfilm, 2017).

- Opposing Verbs
    - Using one word, when you really mean the opposite.
    - "I doused the flames of desire." "Do you mean, you fanned them?" "Yes."
- Vocabulary Slip-ups
    - Using a verb or noun that has a similar meaning, but is more extreme or incorrect.
    - "I burned the spaghetti." "You what?!" "I mean, I *cooked* it!"
- Euphemisms
    - Using a "softer" version of a word to convey meaning without the harshness.
    - "She's passed on." vs. "She's dead."
- Antiphrasis
    - Sarcasm or irony.
    - "I had a *great* time being chased by a hungry bear through the woods."
- Homophones
    - Two or more words that sound the same but have different spellings and meaning
    - "Days of you're" (should be 'yore'.)
- Slang
    - Using a word to convey a concept or feeling.
    - "His outfit is cool." (Not remarking on the number of layers or temperature, but the air of class, presence, attractiveness and novelty the clothing conveys).
- Slurs

- - Using a seemingly innocuous word with the intent of ascribing negative qualities to the person or thing it describes.
  - It's recommended you make up new slurs for your secondary world, as using existing ones may harm or trigger your readership.
- Foreign Loan Words
  - Using a foreign noun to describe a thing that was introduced to your culture from another.
  - For example, the Japanese word for bread is "pan", as bread was first introduced to Japan by the Portuguese.
  - Similarly, the English use "kimono" to describe all traditional Japanese clothing, which directly translates from the Japanese as "thing you wear" or "clothing." But each version of the traditional costume has a specific name. They are not all "kimono", in the same way that calling everything a "dress" doesn't impart the differences between a ball gown and a summer slip.
- Mistranslations or Conflations
  - Scrambling a translation of a word.
  - I will never forget one of my Japanese students telling me that she liked my "neckcessory". She meant my necklace, but had conflated the word with 'accessory' accidentally, and coined the charming term.

As a culture builder, don't forget that all language originates from, and is firmly rooted in, the culture in which it developed. It can grow, change, and adapt, and adopt in foreign loan words. But the cornerstones of its foundation will remain essentially the same.

Thinking of our Fantasy Coastal Town example from earlier, or the Sci-Fi Generational Ship, each culture would have very different ways of using language and common sayings. They may mean the same thing, but the way they're expressed would differ because of the physical and historical context of the home culture.

Don't forget to make sure pieces of your own lived culture don't leak into the language of your make-believe one, if their presence would be jarring. For example, if your world has no France, then there can be no French Fries, French Kisses, or French Braids. Your world can deep-fried tubers, or kisses with open mouths, or can plait hair starting at the crown of the head. But those things would have different names.

Keep that in mind as you work on this next section.

Grammatical Rules

What are the rules for the language that your character speaks? Do they match the way other characters construct sentences?

Formality

Are there more and less formal ways of constructing sentences, or conflating / contracting words? Does everyone use the same level of formality all the time, or does the level of formality change based on the situation and speaker / listener? Does this subtly convey class / race / station / etc. differences by making some characters speak more formally than others in the same situation?

Societal Rules

Are there certain things that certain people can't say? Are some people allowed to ask questions, but others must only speak in statements? Is there a level of vocabulary that is considered crass, and another considered elegant?

Pronunciation

Are all the letters pronounced the same way in each word? Are some letters, or letter combinations, pronounced differently depending on context or where in the word they fall?

Confirmation Bias

Does anyone twist common phrases or idioms to better serve their own agenda? What phrase(s)?

(For example, "Blood is thicker than water" is actually "The blood of the covenant is thicker than the water of the womb." The first version means that you owe loyalty to your family; the second version means that you owe loyalty to those who show you loyalty in return, not to those you are related to, simply because you are related to them.)

Sarcasm and Irony

Does your culture use language to convey an opposite or contrary meaning through word choice and tone? Or is that weird and unnatural to them? How would they respond to meeting someone who *does* use sarcasm?

Lying and Untruths

Similar to the above, does your culture have a concept of binary truth / untruths, and does your culture speak lies or use them? Are there certain situations where lies are allowable and forgivable ("little white lies"), or are they all bad? What are some of the common lies?

Profanity

What are some of their curse words or blasphemous phrases? Who gets to swear? Are there 'replacement' curse words that are more acceptable, like "sugar" for "shit"?

Slurs

In what ways are the undesirable or Othered people described? Are slurs allowed, or are they terribly uncouth and punishable?

Ritual

Is there a common saying or prayer spoken before taking a specific action (like eating, or going into battle)? Is there a stock phrase that people use in specific situations (like the Jewish "May their memory be a blessing" when discussing a dead person.) Is there a phrase used to invoke good luck, or dispel bad luck?

Sayings

In your world, what is:

A saying to mean "take it slow".

A saying to mean "don't take it too slow."

A saying to mean "things will be as they are / things are destined."

A saying to mean "you can fight destiny."

A positive saying about love.

A negative saying about love.

A saying to remind someone of their place in society.

A saying to encourage someone to break out of their place in society.

A saying to encourage someone to honour familial bonds.

A saying that society uses only a part of / misinterprets.

A saying to express condolences.

A saying to express jealousy.

A saying to express joy for another person's successes or achievements.

A saying to express congratulations on a life milestone.

A saying to express a negative opinion of a person.

A saying to express a positive opinion of a person.

WORLDBUILDING THROUGH CULTURE

A saying to compliment a person's ambition.

A saying to deride a person's ambition.

A euphemism for wanting to have sex with someone.

A saying to deride someone for having too much sex.

A saying to deride someone for having too little sex.

A saying to express admiration for a person's beauty.

A saying to express admiration for a person's intelligence.

A saying to express admiration for a person's talent.

A saying to express admiration for a person's bravery.

_____

A saying to express shock or surprise.

_____

A saying to express disappointment.

_____

A saying to blame a higher power for something negative happening.

_____

A saying to praise or thank a higher power for something positive happening.

_____

An expression used to excuse a child's behaviour.

_____

An expression used to excuse misbehaviour.

_____

An expression used to encourage free-thinking.

_____

WORLDBUILDING THROUGH CULTURE

An expression used to encourage a scholar / sports player / warrior to do their best and try hard.

Any other sayings that are useful / often used.

CHARACTER SKETCHES

In this section of the workbook, I've provided you with space to jot down notes about the preferences, influences, and biases that the culture you've created imposes on your characters. As with other sections of the workbook, I encourage you to think thoroughly about each of the choices you make and the answers you write down.

Refer back to the work you've done on earlier pages of when you're setting up the basic personality of your character. Don't just record an answer, also add *why*.

I've also provided space for you to draw, or tape / staple / paste in an image that you feel represents your characters, and will help you remember the details of their physical appearance.

Let your creativity soar!

WORLDBUILDING THROUGH CULTURE

Main Protagonist

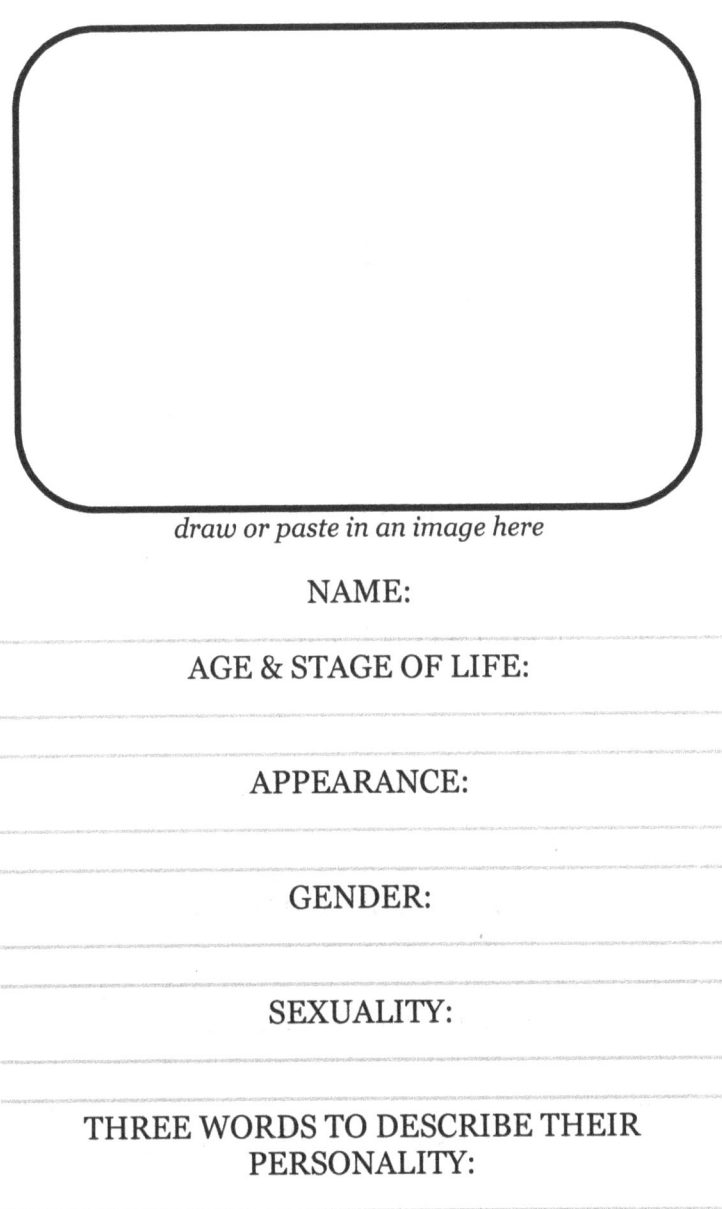

draw or paste in an image here

NAME:

AGE & STAGE OF LIFE:

APPEARANCE:

GENDER:

SEXUALITY:

THREE WORDS TO DESCRIBE THEIR PERSONALITY:

RELATIONSHIPS:

BIGGEST DESIRE / LIFE WISH:

BIGGEST FEAR:

MOST LOVED FOOD & DRINK:

MOST HATED FOOD & DRINK:

MOST EATEN FOOD & DRINK:

MOST LOVED CLOTHES:

MOST HATED CLOTHES:

MOST WORN CLOTHES:

MOST LOVED PLACE:

WORLDBUILDING THROUGH CULTURE

MOST HATED PLACE:

THE PLACE THEY SPEND THE MOST TIME:

RELIGION and / or FAITH & DEVOTEDNESS:

MOST LOVED WAY OF COMMUNICATING:

MOST HATED WAY OF COMMUNICATING:

WHERE THEY GET MOST OF THEIR INFORMATION & THE PROVIDER'S BIAS:

OFTEN USED SAYING OR PHRASE:

IF THEY WERE A COLOUR, THEY WOULD BE:

IF THEY WERE A SONG, THEY WOULD BE:

RELATIONSHIP WITH AUTHORITY:

OTHER NOTES:

Main Antagonist

draw or paste in an image here

NAME:

AGE & STAGE OF LIFE:

APPEARANCE:

GENDER:

SEXUALITY:

THREE WORDS TO DESCRIBE THEIR PERSONALITY:

WORLDBUILDING THROUGH CULTURE

RELATIONSHIPS:

BIGGEST DESIRE / LIFE WISH:

BIGGEST FEAR:

MOST LOVED FOOD & DRINK:

MOST HATED FOOD & DRINK:

MOST EATEN FOOD & DRINK:

MOST LOVED CLOTHES:

MOST HATED CLOTHES:

MOST WORN CLOTHES:

MOST LOVED PLACE:

MOST HATED PLACE:

THE PLACE THEY SPEND THE MOST TIME:

RELIGION and / or FAITH & DEVOTEDNESS:

MOST LOVED WAY OF COMMUNICATING:

MOST HATED WAY OF COMMUNICATING:

WHERE THEY GET MOST OF THEIR INFORMATION & THE PROVIDER'S BIAS:

OFTEN USED SAYING OR PHRASE:

IF THEY WERE A COLOUR, THEY WOULD BE:

IF THEY WERE A SONG, THEY WOULD BE:

RELATIONSHIP WITH AUTHORITY:

OTHER NOTES:

WORLDBUILDING THROUGH CULTURE

SECONDARY CHARACTER

draw or paste in an image here

NAME:

AGE & STAGE OF LIFE:

APPEARANCE:

GENDER:

SEXUALITY:

THREE WORDS TO DESCRIBE THEIR PERSONALITY:

RELATIONSHIPS:

BIGGEST DESIRE / LIFE WISH:

BIGGEST FEAR:

MOST LOVED FOOD & DRINK:

MOST HATED FOOD & DRINK:

MOST EATEN FOOD & DRINK:

MOST LOVED CLOTHES:

MOST HATED CLOTHES:

MOST WORN CLOTHES:

MOST LOVED PLACE:

WORLDBUILDING THROUGH CULTURE

MOST HATED PLACE:

THE PLACE THEY SPEND THE MOST TIME:

RELIGION and / or FAITH & DEVOTEDNESS:

MOST LOVED WAY OF COMMUNICATING:

MOST HATED WAY OF COMMUNICATING:

WHERE THEY GET MOST OF THEIR INFORMATION & THE PROVIDER'S BIAS:

OFTEN USED SAYING OR PHRASE:

IF THEY WERE A COLOUR, THEY WOULD BE:

IF THEY WERE A SONG, THEY WOULD BE:

RELATIONSHIP WITH AUTHORITY:

OTHER NOTES:

J.M. FREY

SECONDARY CHARACTER

draw or paste in an image here

NAME:

AGE & STAGE OF LIFE:

APPEARANCE:

GENDER:

SEXUALITY:

THREE WORDS TO DESCRIBE THEIR PERSONALITY:

WORLDBUILDING THROUGH CULTURE

RELATIONSHIPS:

BIGGEST DESIRE / LIFE WISH:

BIGGEST FEAR:

MOST LOVED FOOD & DRINK:

MOST HATED FOOD & DRINK:

MOST EATEN FOOD & DRINK:

MOST LOVED CLOTHES:

MOST HATED CLOTHES:

MOST WORN CLOTHES:

MOST LOVED PLACE:

MOST HATED PLACE:

THE PLACE THEY SPEND THE MOST TIME:

RELIGION and / or FAITH & DEVOTEDNESS:

MOST LOVED WAY OF COMMUNICATING:

MOST HATED WAY OF COMMUNICATING:

WHERE THEY GET MOST OF THEIR INFORMATION & THE PROVIDER'S BIAS:

OFTEN USED SAYING OR PHRASE:

IF THEY WERE A COLOUR, THEY WOULD BE:

IF THEY WERE A SONG, THEY WOULD BE:

RELATIONSHIP WITH AUTHORITY:

OTHER NOTES:

WORLDBUILDING THROUGH CULTURE

Secondary Character

draw or paste in an image here

NAME:

AGE & STAGE OF LIFE:

APPEARANCE:

GENDER:

SEXUALITY:

THREE WORDS TO DESCRIBE THEIR PERSONALITY:

RELATIONSHIPS:

BIGGEST DESIRE / LIFE WISH:

BIGGEST FEAR:

MOST LOVED FOOD & DRINK:

MOST HATED FOOD & DRINK:

MOST EATEN FOOD & DRINK:

MOST LOVED CLOTHES:

MOST HATED CLOTHES:

MOST WORN CLOTHES:

MOST LOVED PLACE:

WORLDBUILDING THROUGH CULTURE

MOST HATED PLACE:

THE PLACE THEY SPEND THE MOST TIME:

RELIGION and / or FAITH & DEVOTEDNESS:

MOST LOVED WAY OF COMMUNICATING:

MOST HATED WAY OF COMMUNICATING:

WHERE THEY GET MOST OF THEIR INFORMATION & THE PROVIDER'S BIAS:

OFTEN USED SAYING OR PHRASE:

IF THEY WERE A COLOUR, THEY WOULD BE:

IF THEY WERE A SONG, THEY WOULD BE:

RELATIONSHIP WITH AUTHORITY:

OTHER NOTES:

J.M. FREY

Secondary Character

draw or paste in an image here

NAME:

AGE & STAGE OF LIFE:

APPEARANCE:

GENDER:

SEXUALITY:

THREE WORDS TO DESCRIBE THEIR PERSONALITY:

WORLDBUILDING THROUGH CULTURE

RELATIONSHIPS:

BIGGEST DESIRE / LIFE WISH:

BIGGEST FEAR:

MOST LOVED FOOD & DRINK:

MOST HATED FOOD & DRINK:

MOST EATEN FOOD & DRINK:

MOST LOVED CLOTHES:

MOST HATED CLOTHES:

MOST WORN CLOTHES:

MOST LOVED PLACE:

MOST HATED PLACE:

THE PLACE THEY SPEND THE MOST TIME:

RELIGION and / or FAITH & DEVOTEDNESS:

MOST LOVED WAY OF COMMUNICATING:

MOST HATED WAY OF COMMUNICATING:

WHERE THEY GET MOST OF THEIR INFORMATION & THE PROVIDER'S BIAS:

OFTEN USED SAYING OR PHRASE:

IF THEY WERE A COLOUR, THEY WOULD BE:

IF THEY WERE A SONG, THEY WOULD BE:

RELATIONSHIP WITH AUTHORITY:

OTHER NOTES:

WORLDBUILDING THROUGH CULTURE

SECONDARY CHARACTER

draw or paste in an image here

NAME:

AGE & STAGE OF LIFE:

APPEARANCE:

GENDER:

SEXUALITY:

THREE WORDS TO DESCRIBE THEIR PERSONALITY:

RELATIONSHIPS:

BIGGEST DESIRE / LIFE WISH:

BIGGEST FEAR:

MOST LOVED FOOD & DRINK:

MOST HATED FOOD & DRINK:

MOST EATEN FOOD & DRINK:

MOST LOVED CLOTHES:

MOST HATED CLOTHES:

MOST WORN CLOTHES:

MOST LOVED PLACE:

WORLDBUILDING THROUGH CULTURE

MOST HATED PLACE:

THE PLACE THEY SPEND THE MOST TIME:

RELIGION and / or FAITH & DEVOTEDNESS:

MOST LOVED WAY OF COMMUNICATING:

MOST HATED WAY OF COMMUNICATING:

WHERE THEY GET MOST OF THEIR INFORMATION & THE PROVIDER'S BIAS:

OFTEN USED SAYING OR PHRASE:

IF THEY WERE A COLOUR, THEY WOULD BE:

IF THEY WERE A SONG, THEY WOULD BE:

RELATIONSHIP WITH AUTHORITY:

OTHER NOTES:

SECONDARY CHARACTER

draw or paste in an image here

NAME:

AGE & STAGE OF LIFE:

APPEARANCE:

GENDER:

SEXUALITY:

THREE WORDS TO DESCRIBE THEIR PERSONALITY:

WORLDBUILDING THROUGH CULTURE

RELATIONSHIPS:

BIGGEST DESIRE / LIFE WISH:

BIGGEST FEAR:

MOST LOVED FOOD & DRINK:

MOST HATED FOOD & DRINK:

MOST EATEN FOOD & DRINK:

MOST LOVED CLOTHES:

MOST HATED CLOTHES:

MOST WORN CLOTHES:

MOST LOVED PLACE:

MOST HATED PLACE:

THE PLACE THEY SPEND THE MOST TIME:

RELIGION and / or FAITH & DEVOTEDNESS:

MOST LOVED WAY OF COMMUNICATING:

MOST HATED WAY OF COMMUNICATING:

WHERE THEY GET MOST OF THEIR INFORMATION & THE PROVIDER'S BIAS:

OFTEN USED SAYING OR PHRASE:

IF THEY WERE A COLOUR, THEY WOULD BE:

IF THEY WERE A SONG, THEY WOULD BE:

RELATIONSHIP WITH AUTHORITY:

OTHER NOTES:

NOTES

WORLDBUILDING THROUGH CULTURE

WORLDBUILDING THROUGH CULTURE

WORLDBUILDING THROUGH CULTURE

WORLDBUILDING THROUGH CULTURE

WORLDBUILDING THROUGH CULTURE

WORLDBUILDING THROUGH CULTURE

WORLDBUILDING THROUGH CULTURE

WORLDBUILDING THROUGH CULTURE

ABOUT THE AUTHOR

J.M. Frey is an award-winning author and lapsed academic.

With an MA in Communications and Culture, she's appeared on podcasts, in documentaries, and on radio and television.
Her life's ambition is to have stepped foot on every continent
(only 3 left!)

J.M. is also a professionally trained actor who takes absolute delight in weird stories, over the top performances, and quirky characters. She's played everything from Marmee to the Red Queen, Annie to Jane Eyre, and strange creatures, curious young boys, and earnest heroines as a voice actor.

www.jmfrey.net
Author Photo by Marion Voysey

ALSO BY J.M. FREY

(Back)
Triptych
The Dark Lord and the Seamstress, a colouring storybook
"The Promise" in *Valor 2*
Hero Is A Four Letter Word, short story collection
"Whose Doctor?" in *Doctor Who In Time And Space: Essays on Themes, Characters, History and Fandom, 1963–2012*
"How Fanfiction Made Me Gay," in *The Secret Loves of Geek Girls*
"Time to Move," in *The Secret Loves of Geek Girls Redux*
"Bloodsuckers" and "Toronto the Rude" in *The Toronto Comic Anthology vol 2*
City By Night
"TTC Gothic" in *Amazing Stories vols 1-4*
The Woman Who Fell Through Time
Lips Like Ice, as Peggy Barnett

The Accidental Turn Series
The Untold Tale
The Forgotten Tale
The Silenced Tale
The Accidental Collection, short stories and novellas

The Skylark's Saga
The Skylark's Song
The Skylark's Sacrifice

www.ingramcontent.com/pod-product-compliance
Lightning Source LLC
Chambersburg PA
CBHW012000090526
44590CB00026B/3801